The Observer's Pocket Series

AIRCRAFT

The Observer Books

A POCKET REFERENCE SERIES
COVERING NATURAL HISTORY, TRANSPORT,
THE ARTS ETC

Natural History

BIRDS
BIRDS' EGGS
BUTTERFLIES
LARGER MOTHS
COMMON INSECTS
WILD ANIMALS
ZOO ANIMALS
WILD FLOWERS
GARDEN FLOWERS
FLOWERING TREES
  AND SHRUBS
CACTI
TREES
GRASSES
FERNS
COMMON FUNGI
LICHENS
POND LIFE
FRESHWATER FISHES
SEA FISHES
SEA AND SEASHORE
GEOLOGY
ASTRONOMY
WEATHER
CATS
DOGS
HORSES AND PONIES

Transport

AIRCRAFT
AUTOMOBILES
COMMERCIAL VEHICLES
SHIPS
MANNED SPACEFLIGHT

The Arts etc

ARCHITECTURE
CATHEDRALS
CHURCHES
HERALDRY
FLAGS
PAINTING
MODERN ART
SCULPTURE
FURNITURE
POTTERY AND
  PORCELAIN
MUSIC
POSTAGE STAMPS

Sport

ASSOCIATION FOOTBALL
CRICKET

Cities

LONDON

The Observer's Book of
AIRCRAFT

COMPILED BY

WILLIAM GREEN

WITH SILHOUETTES BY

DENNIS PUNNETT

DESCRIBING 137 AIRCRAFT
WITH 246 ILLUSTRATIONS

1974 Edition

FREDERICK WARNE & CO LTD
FREDERICK WARNE & CO INC
LONDON · NEW YORK

© FREDERICK WARNE & CO LTD
LONDON, ENGLAND
1974

Twenty-third Edition 1974

LIBRARY OF CONGRESS CATALOG CARD NO: 57–4425

ISBN 0 7232 1526 X

Printed in Great Britain

INTRODUCTION TO THE 1974 EDITION

With the passing for press of this, the 23rd annual edition of *The Observer's Book of Aircraft*, it is interesting if sad to reflect that during this score-and-three years there has been no twelvemonth in which aerial warfare has not been recorded somewhere in the world. The year now past was certainly no exception as it encompassed the October Middle East conflict; small wonder, therefore, that substantially more than half the content matter of this volume is devoted to aircraft possessing purely military roles, despite the fact that 1974 does not promise to be particularly proliferous in the new military aircraft types to which it will give birth. However, few though these newcomers may be in number, their singular interest could well promote this year to the vintage category.

The first of these débutantes will be the multi-national Panavia multi-role combat aircraft, or MRCA (see page 162), which is of vital importance in the future planning of the RAF, the Federal German *Luftwaffe* and Italy's *Aeronautica Militare*. Sharing variable geometry with the MRCA but rather more spectacular in view of its size will be the Rockwell B-1A strategic bomber (see page 172), which is comparable from some aspects with the Soviet Union's *Backfire*, also taking its place in the *Observer's Book* for the first time with this edition. Another innovative military aircraft to commence its test programme during the coming summer is the Rockwell XFV-12A (see page 174), an advanced technology development aircraft and potential forerunner of a shipboard fighter and attack aircraft which will be preceded into the air in the USA by the YF-16 and YF-17 fighters (see pages 88 and 158 respectively), created in an attempt to arrest the upward cost spiral bedevilling fighter development and, for that matter, all other military aircraft development programmes.

The more interesting civil newcomers appearing for the first time include the Canadian DHC-7 STOL short-haul transport (see page 72), the world's first *turbojet*-driven biplane in the form of the M-15 agricultural aircraft from the WSK-Mielec (see page 220), and the Tu-144 long-range supersonic transport which, in the form illustrated, differs so radically from the prototypes illustrated in previous editions as to constitute virtually a *new* aeroplane.

For the benefit of newer readers, it should perhaps be mentioned that the *Observer's Book* is intended to present in compact form each year the new aircraft types and variants of existing types that have made their début during the preceding twelve months and may be expected to appear during the year of currency of the volume. Those readers requiring details of the aircraft that they are most likely to see and which, numerically, are among the most important, are recommended to the companion *Observer's Basic Aircraft Directories*, these two volumes (one devoted to civil and the other to military aircraft) having now been re-issued in completely revised and updated form and in enlarged format.

WILLIAM GREEN

AERITALIA-AERMACCHI AM-3C

Country of Origin: Italy.
Type: Battlefield surveillance and forward air control aircraft.
Power Plant: One 340 hp Piaggio-built Avco Lycoming GSO-480-B1B6 six-cylinder horizontally-opposed engine.
Performance: (At 3,307 lb/1 500 kg) Max. speed, 161 mph (260 km/h) at sea level, 173 mph (278 km/h) at 8,000 ft (2 440 m); max. cruise, 153 mph (246 km/h) at 8,000 ft (2 440 m); max. range (with 30 min reserves), 615 mls (990 km); initial climb, 1,378 ft/min (7,0 m/sec).
Weights: Empty equipped, 2,535 lb (1149 kg); normal loaded, 3,307 lb (1 500 kg); max. take-off, 3,858 lb (1 750 kg).
Armament: Four underwing hardpoints for various ordnance loads. Two inner hardpoints stressed for 375 lb (170 kg) and two outer hardpoints stressed for 200 lb (91 kg). Armament options include four LAU-32A or Matra 181 rocket launchers, 12 80-mm SURA rockets, two Nord AS.11 missiles, two 7,62-mm Minigun pods, or two 250-lb (113,4-kg) and two 200-lb (91-kg) bombs.
Accommodation: Pilot and co-pilot/observer in tandem.
Status: First of two flying prototypes flown May 12, 1967, followed by second on August 22, 1968. First production example flown mid-1972 with initial deliveries (against order for 40 from South Africa) initiated mid-1973.
Notes: Three ordered by Rwanda and order for 20 for use in training role anticipated from Italian Army.

AERITALIA-AERMACCHI AM-3C

Dimensions: Span, 41 ft $5\frac{1}{3}$ in (12,64 m); length, 29 ft $10\frac{1}{8}$ in (9,09 m); height, 8 ft 11 in (2,72 m); wing area, 219·15 sq ft (20,36 m²).

AERITALIA (FIAT) G.222

Country of Origin: Italy.
Type: General-purpose military transport.
Power Plant: Two 2,970 shp General Electric CT64-820 turboprops. (Production) Two 3,400 shp T64-P4D turboprops.
Performance: (Estimated with T64-P4D engines) Max. speed, 329 mph (530 km/h) at sea level; normal cruise, 273 mph (440 km/h) at 14,750 ft (4 500 m); range with 11,025-lb (5 000-kg) payload, 1,920 mls (3 250 km), with max. fuel, 3,262 mls (5 250 km); max. initial climb rate, 1,890 ft/min (9,6 m/sec).
Weights: Empty, 29,320 lb (13 300 kg); empty equipped, 32,408 lb (14 700 kg); max. take-off, 57,320 lb (26 000 kg).
Accommodation: Flight crew of three or four and seats for 44 fully-equipped troops or 40 paratroops. Alternative loads include 36 casualty stretchers, two jeep-type vehicles or equivalent freight.
Status: First of two prototypes flown July 18, 1970, followed by second prototype on July 22, 1971, and work had begun on six pre-production examples at the beginning of 1973. An order for 44 aircraft for the Italian Air Force was placed on July 28, 1972, and it is anticipated that deliveries of the G.222 will commence during the course of 1975.
Notes: Prototypes powered by CT64-820 turboprops and unpressurised, but the programmed production model will have uprated T64-P4D turboprops and provision for pressurisation. The G.222 is intended as a successor to some of the Italian Air Force's ageing Fairchild C-119 transports. Current planning calls for the G.222 to equip two squadrons of the Italian Air Force.

AERITALIA (FIAT) G.222

Dimensions: Span, 94 ft 5¾ in (28,80 m); length, 74 ft 5½ in (22,70 m); height, 32 ft 1¾ in (9,80 m); wing area, 970·9 sq ft (90,2 m²).

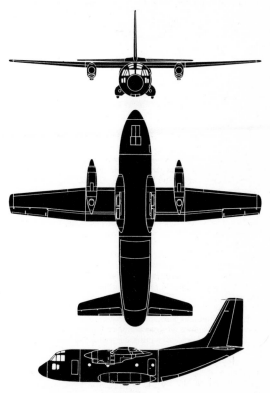

AERMACCHI M.B.326K

Country of Origin: Italy.

Type: Single-seat operational trainer and close-support aircraft.

Power Plant: One 4,000 lb (1 814 kg) Rolls-Royce Viper 632-43 turbojet.

Performance: (Estimated) Max. speed without external stores, 550 mph (885 km/h) at 19,685 ft (6 000 m); max. cruise, 497 mph (800 km/h); ferry range with two 90 Imp. gal. (409 l) underwing auxiliary tanks, 1,400 mls (2 250 km).

Weights: Empty equipped, 6,298 lb (2 857 kg); loaded (clean), 9,678 lb (4 390 kg); max., 12,000 lb (5 443 kg).

Armament: Two 30-mm DEFA or Aden cannon with 150 rpg. Six underwing stores stations of which four stressed for loads up to 1,000 lb (453,5 kg) and two for loads up to 750 lb (340 kg). Max. external ordnance load of 4,500 lb (2 040 kg).

Status: First prototype M.B.326K flown August 22, 1970 with Viper 540 turbojet and second prototype with Viper 632 flown May 21, 1971. Flight test programme completed during 1972 with production deliveries (against initial batch of 20 for South Africa) commencing mid-1973.

Notes: M.B.326K is a single-seat dual-purpose derivative of the two-seat M.B.326G with the 3,410 lb (1 547 kg) Viper 540 turbojet (see 1970 edition). Apart from a more powerful turbojet, built-in cannon armament and a single-seat cockpit, the M.B.326K embodies some local strengthening of the forward fuselage structure, a high-flotation undercarriage, and provision for armour protection. Assembly in South Africa is scheduled to commence in 1974 against reported requirement for 100 aircraft.

AERMACCHI M.B.326K

Dimensions: Span (over tip tanks), 35 ft 6$\frac{3}{4}$ in (10,84 m); length, 34 ft 10$\frac{7}{8}$ in (10,64 m); height, 12 ft 1$\frac{3}{4}$ in (3,70 m); wing area, 207·958 sq ft (19,32 m²).

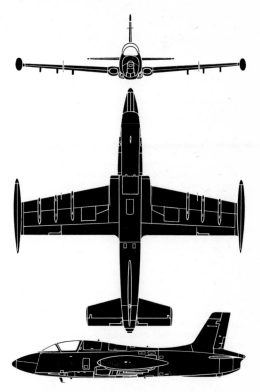

AERO L 39 ALBATROSS

Country of Origin: Czechoslovakia.
Type: Tandem two-seat basic and advanced trainer.
Power Plant: One 3,784 lb (1 715 kg) Walter Titan (Ivchenko AI-25TL) turbofan.
Performance: Max. speed (at 9,039 lb/4 100 kg), 466 mph (750 km/h) at 16,400 ft (5 000 m), 385 mph (620 km/h) at sea level; range on internal fuel with 5% reserves, 680 mls (1 100 km), with tip-tanks and no reserves, 930 mls (1 500 km); initial climb, 4,348 ft/min (22,9 m/sec); ceiling, 34,510 ft (11 300 m).
Weights: Empty, 6,283 lb (2 850 kg); normal take-off, 9,039 lb (4 100 kg).
Armament: Two wing hard points for gun or rocket pods, or (L 39Z) four wing hard points for ASMs, 16-rocket pods or 20-mm cannon pods.
Status: First of five flying prototypes flown on November 4, 1968, and first of pre-production batch of 10 aircraft joined test programme during 1971. Initial production aircraft completed late 1972 with full production initiated late 1973 after adoption as standard trainer by the Warsaw Pact nations (with the exception of Poland).
Notes: The L 39 is intended as a successor for the L 29 Delfin and, after protracted evaluation, was adopted in 1973, production being expected to exceed 2,000 aircraft and to stretch over 8–10 years. Military qualification trials were completed in the Soviet Union during 1973, and an armed version, the L 39Z for the light strike role, is being developed for export, the first designated customer being Iraq.

12

AERO L 39 ALBATROSS

Dimensions: Span, 30 ft 10 in (9,40 m); length, 40 ft 4$\frac{1}{4}$ in (12,30 m); height, 15 ft 4$\frac{1}{2}$ in (4,70 m); wing area, 202·4 sq ft (18,8 m^2).

AÉROSPATIALE CORVETTE 100

Country of Origin: France.
Type: Light business executive transport.
Power Plant: Two 2,310 lb (1 048 kg) Pratt & Whitney
JT15D-4 turbofans.
Performance: Max. cruise at 12,125 lb (5 500 kg), 495 mph
(796 km/h) at 29,530 ft (9 000 m), at 13,448 lb (6 100 kg),
483 mph (778 km/h) at 25,000 ft (7 620 m); econ. cruise,
385 mph (620 km/h) at 36,090 ft (11 000 m); max. range
on internal fuel, 913 mls (1 470 km) at econ. cruise with
reserves for 45 min hold at 5,000 ft (1 520 m), with optional
77 Imp gal (350 l) wingtip tanks, 1,520 mls (2 445 km);
max. climb, 3,000 ft/min (15,25 m/sec).
Weights: Empty equipped, 7,985 lb (3 622 kg); max. take-
off, 13,448 lb (6 100 kg).
Accommodation: Crew of one or two on flight deck plus
4–6 passengers in executive version. Standard arrangements for 8, 10 or 12 passengers and aeromedical arrangement for three stretchers and two medical attendants.
Status: Prototype (SN 600) flown July 16, 1970, followed
by first of two pre-series aircraft (SN 601) on December 20,
1972. First of initial production series of five flown November
9, 1973, with production rate of two per month late 1974.
Notes: A projected development of the Corvette 100 is the
Corvette 200 with a 6·56-ft (2,0-m) fuselage stretch permitting accommodation of up to 18 passengers. A further
projected derivative is the scaled-up three-engined Corvette
300.

AÉROSPATIALE CORVETTE 100

Dimensions: Span, 41 ft 11⅞ in (12,80 m), with tip tanks, 43 ft 5¼ in (13,24 m); length, 45 ft 4 in (13,82 m); height, 13 ft 10 in (4,23 m); wing area, 236·8 sq ft (22,00 m²).

15

AÉROSPATIALE RALLYE 180 GT

Country of Origin: France.
Type: Light cabin monoplane.
Power Plant: One 180 hp Lycoming O-360-A3A four-cylinder horizontally-opposed engine.
Performance: Max. speed, 150 mph (240 km/h) at sea level; cruise at 75% power, 140 mph (225 km/h); normal range, 575 mls (925 km/h); initial climb rate, 787 ft/min (4,0 m/sec); service ceiling, 12,800 ft (3 900 m).
Weights: Empty equipped, 1,212 lb (550 kg); max. take-off, 2,315 lb (1 050 kg).
Accommodation: Two individual seats in front with dual controls and bench seat for two persons at the rear.
Status: The Rallye 180 GT is the 1973 production version of the MS 893 Rallye Commodore 180, first flown in prototype form on December 7, 1964, and in continuous production since 1965. Total Rallye production exceeded 2,300 by the beginning of 1974.
Notes: The 1974 range of Rallye light monoplanes manufactured by the Aviation Générale Division of Aérospatiale comprises, in addition to the Rallye 180 GT, the Rallye 100 (100 hp Rolls-Royce/Continental O-200-A), the Rallye 125 (125 hp Lycoming O-235-F2A), the Rallye 150 GT (150 hp Lycoming O-320-E2A), and the Rallye 220 GT (220 hp Franklin 6A-350-C1), the last-mentioned being illustrated above. The GT (*Grand Tourisme*) models introduce a number of changes, such as a wheel in place of control stick and a central console for engine controls, but the airframes of all versions are essentially similar.

AÉROSPATIALE RALLYE 180 GT

Dimensions: Span, 31 ft 6¼ in (9,61 m); length, 23 ft 5¾ in (7,16 m); height, 9 ft 2¼ in (2,80 m); wing area, 132 sq ft (12,30 m²).

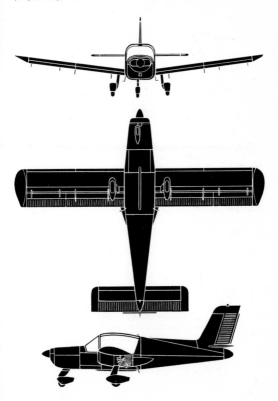

AIRBUS A300B2

Country of Origin: International consortium.

Type: Short- to medium-range commercial transport.

Power Plant: Two 49,000 lb (22 260 kg) General Electric CF6-50A or (from 1975) 51,000 lb (23 133 kg) CF6-50C turbofans.

Performance: Max. cruise, 582 mph (937 km/h) at 25,000 ft (7 620 m); typical high-speed cruise, 570 mph (917 km/h) at 30,000 ft (9 145 m); typical long-range cruise, 526 mph (847 km/h) at 31,000 ft (9 450 m); range with 281 passengers, 1,615 mls (2 600 km), with max. fuel, 2,300 mls (3 700 km).

Weights: Typical operational empty, 186,810 lb (84 740 kg); max. take-off, 302,032 lb (137 000 kg).

Accommodation: Basic flight crew of three and basic arrangement for 281 passengers with high-density arrangement for 345 passengers.

Status: First and second A300Bs (dimensionally to B1 standard) flown October 28, 1972, and February 5, 1973, respectively, with third A300B (to B2 standard) flying on June 28, 1973. First of seven A300B2s (plus nine on option) for Air France scheduled for March 1974 delivery with deliveries of three (with four on option) to Lufthansa commencing 1975. Current orders for 18 (and options on 21), including longer-range A300B4 (for Iberia and Sterling). Nine scheduled to be produced in 1974 and 30 in 1975.

Notes: The A300B is being manufactured by an international consortium comprising Aérospatiale (France), Deutsche Airbus (Federal Germany), Hawker Siddeley (UK), CASA (Spain) and Fokker-VFW (Netherlands), the programme being managed by Airbus Industrie. The A300B1 (illustrated above) has a 167 ft $2\frac{1}{4}$ in (50,97 m) fuselage, and the longer-range A300B4 will have a 330,700 lb (150 000 kg) gross weight.

AIRBUS A300B2

Dimensions: Span, 147 ft $1\frac{1}{4}$ in (44,84 m); length, 175 ft 11 in (53,62 m); height, 54 ft 2 in (16,53 m); wing area, 2,799 sq ft (260,0 m²).

ANTONOV AN-26 (CURL)

Country of Origin: USSR.

Type: Short- to medium-range military and commercial freighter.

Power Plant: Two 2,820 eshp Ivchenko AI-24T turboprops and one (starboard nacelle) 1,984 lb (900 kg) Tumansky RU-19-300 auxiliary turbojet.

Performance: Max. speed, 335 mph (540 km/h) at 19,685 ft (6 000 m); normal cruise, 280 mph (450 km/h) at 19,685 ft (6 000 m); range cruise, 273 mph (440 km/h) at 22,965 ft (7 000 m); range with 3,307 lb (1 500 kg) payload and reserves, 1,553 mls (2 500 km), with 11,023 lb (5 000 kg) payload and reserves, 808 mls (1 300 km); service ceiling, 24,935 ft (7 600 m).

Weights: Empty equipped, 37,258 lb (16 914 kg); max. take-off, 52,911 lb (24 000 kg).

Accommodation: Normal crew of five with folding seats for up to 38 passengers/troops along main cabin walls. Direct rear loading for freight or vehicles and provision for air-dropping over rear ramp.

Status: Production deliveries for both military and commercial use reportedly commenced 1969.

Notes: Derivative of the commercial An-24RT intended for both military and civil applications, the An-26 differs from An-24 variants in having a completely redesigned rear fuselage of "beavertail" type, and large paradrop observation blister to port below and aft of the flight deck. Structurally, the An-26 is essentially similar to the An-24 Series II (see 1969 edition), and has an auxiliary turbojet in the starboard nacelle as introduced by the An-24RT. A photographic survey derivative of the An-24 with an extensively glazed and redesigned nose is designated An-30.

ANTONOV AN-26 (CURL)

Dimensions: Span, 95 ft 10 in (29,20 m); length, 78 ft 1 in (23,80 m); height, 28 ft 1$\frac{2}{3}$ in (8,57 m); wing area, 779·95 sq ft (72,46 m²).

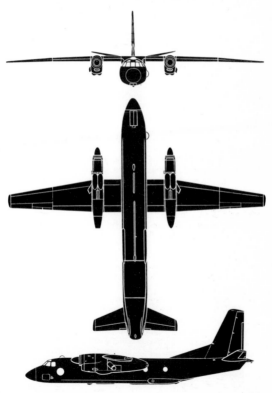

BAC 167 STRIKEMASTER

Country of Origin: United Kingdom.

Type: Side-by-side two-seat basic trainer and light attack and counter-insurgency aircraft.

Power Plant: One 3,410 lb (1 547 kg) Rolls-Royce Viper 535 turbojet.

Performance: Max. speed, 450 mph (724 km/h) at sea level, 472 mph (760 km/h) at 20,000 ft (6 096 m); range at 8,355 lb (3 789 kg), 725 mls (1 166 km), at 10,500 lb (4 762 kg), 1,238 mls (1 992 km), at 11,500 lb (5 216 kg), 1,382 mls (2 224 km); initial climb at 8,355 lb (3 789 kg), 5,250 ft/min (26,67 m/sec); time to 30,000 ft (9 150 m), 8 min 45 sec, to 40,000 ft (12 200 m), 15 min 30 sec.

Weights: Empty equipped, 5,850 lb (2 653 kg); normal take-off (pilot training), 8,355 lb (3 789 kg), (navigational training), 9,143 lb (4 147 kg); max., 11,500 lb (5 216 kg).

Armament: Provision for two 7,62-mm FN machine guns with 550 rpg and eight underwing stores stations for up to 3,000 lb (1 360 kg) of stores.

Status: Prototype Strikemaster flown October 26, 1967, with production deliveries following late 1968. Versions ordered and which differ only in equipment specified include Mk. 80 (Saudi Arabia), Mk. 81 (South Yemen), Mk. 82 (Muscat and Oman), Mk. 83 (Kuwait), Mk. 84 (Singapore), Mk. 87 (Kenya), Mk. 88 (New Zealand) and Mk. 89 (Ecuador). Total of 115 Strikemasters contracted for by beginning of 1974 when limited production was continuing.

Notes: Derivative of the externally similar BAC 145 Jet Provost T. Mk. 5 (see 1971 edition) from which it differs primarily in having a more powerful engine, some local structural strengthening, and additional stores stations. Total of 110 Jet Provost T. Mk. 5s delivered to the RAF.

22

BAC 167 STRIKEMASTER

Dimensions: Span, 35 ft 4 in (10,77 m); length, 34 ft 0 in (10,36 m); height, 10 ft 2 in (3,10 m); wing area, 213·7 sq ft (19,80 m²).

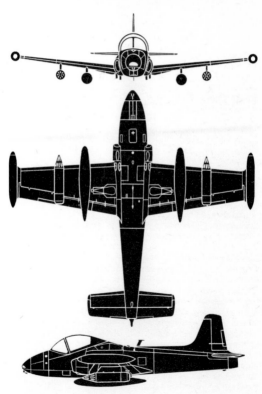

BAC ONE-ELEVEN 475

Country of Origin: United Kingdom.
Type: Short- to medium-range commercial transport.
Power Plant: Two 12,550 lb (5 692 kg) Rolls-Royce Spey 512-14-DW turbofans.
Performance: Max. cruise, 548 mph (882 km/h) at 21,000 ft (6 400 m); econ. cruise, 507 mph (815 km/h) at 25,000 ft (7 620 m); range with reserves for 230 mls (370 km) diversion and 45 min, 2,095 mls (3 370 km), with capacity payload, 1,590 mls (2 560 km); initial climb rate at 345 mph (555 km/h), 2,350 ft/min (11,93 m/sec).
Weights: Basic operational, 51,814 lb (23 502 kg); max. take-off, 92,000 lb (41 730 kg).
Accommodation: Basic flight crew of two and up to 89 passengers. Typical mixed-class arrangement provides for 16 first-class (four-abreast) and 49 tourist-class (five-abreast) passengers.
Status: Aerodynamic prototype of One-Eleven 475 flown August 27, 1970 followed by first production model on April 5, 1971, with certification and first production deliveries following in June. Total of 210 examples of all versions of the One-Eleven ordered by beginning of 1974.
Notes: The One-Eleven 475 combines the standard fuselage of the Series 400 with the redesigned wing and uprated engines of the Series 500 (see 1970 edition), coupling these with a low-pressure undercarriage to permit operation from gravel or low-strength sealed runways. The One-Eleven prototype flew on August 20, 1963, production models including the physically similar Series 200 and 300 with 10,330 lb (4 686 kg) Spey 506s and 11,400 lb (5 170 kg) Spey 511s, the Series 400 modified for US operation, and the Series 500 which is similar to the 475 apart from the fuselage and undercarriage.

BAC ONE-ELEVEN 475

Dimensions: Span, 93 ft 6 in (28,50 m); length, 93 ft 6 in (28,50 m); height, 24 ft 6 in (7,47 m); wing area, 1,031 sq ft (95,78 m²).

BAC-AÉROSPATIALE CONCORDE

Countries of Origin: United Kingdom and France.

Type: Long-range supersonic commercial transport.

Power Plant: Four 38,050 lb (17 259 kg) reheat Rolls-Royce/SNECMA Olympus 593 Mk. 602 turbojets.

Performance: Max. cruise, 1,450 mph (2 330 km/h) or Mach 2·2 at 54,500 ft (16 000 m); max. range cruise, 1,350 mph (2 170 km/h) or Mach 2·05; max. fuel range with FAR reserves and 17,000-lb (7 710-kg) payload, 4,400 mls (7 080 km); max. payload range, 3,600 mls (5 790 km) at 616 mph (990 km/h) or Mach 0·93 at 30,000 ft (9 100 m), 4,020 mls (6 470 km) at 1,350 mph (2 170 km/h) or Mach 2·05 at 54,500 ft (16 000 m); initial climb, 5,000 ft/min (25,4 m/sec).

Weights: Operational empty, 169,000 lb (76 650 kg); max. take-off, 385,810 lb (175 000 kg).

Accommodation: Normal flight crew of three and economy-class seating for 128 passengers. Alternative high-density arrangement for 144 passengers.

Status: First and second prototypes flown March 2 and April 9, 1969 respectively. First of two pre-production aircraft flew December 17, 1971, the second (illustrated above) flying on January 10, 1973. The first production aircraft was flown on December 6, 1973, and was to be joined by the second in January 1974.

Notes: Both specification and general-arrangement silhouette apply to production Concorde, the prototypes featuring a shorter fuselage and differences in cockpit visor and wing profile. The Concorde reached Mach 2·0 on November 4, 1970, the prototypes having 34,700 lb (15 740 kg) Olympus 593-3Bs, and the definitive engine for the production model will be the Olympus 612 of 39,940 lb (18 116 kg). Fifteen production Concordes were under construction by beginning of 1974 (plus long lead time items for six more).

BAC-AÉROSPATIALE CONCORDE

Dimensions: Span, 84 ft 0 in (25,60 m); length, 203 ft 8¾ in (62,10 m); height, 39 ft 10¼ in (12,15 m); wing area, 3,856 sq ft (358,25 m²).

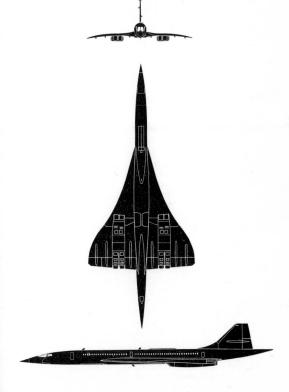

BEECHCRAFT B99

Country of Origin: USA.

Type: Light commercial feederliner.

Power Plant: Two 680 shp Pratt & Whitney PT6A-28 turboprops.

Performance: Max. cruise, 284 mph (457 km/h) at 12,000 ft (3 650 m); econ. cruise, 279 mph (449 km/h) at 8,000 ft (2 440 m); range cruise, 216 mph (348 km/h) at 8,000 ft (2 440 m); max. fuel range, 887 mls (1 427 km) at 8,000 ft (2 440 m) with 45 min reserves at 279 mph (449 km/h), 1,048 mls (1 686 km) at 216 mph (348 km/h).

Weights: Empty equipped (standard 15-seater), 5,780 lb (2 621 kg); max. take-off, 10,900 lb (4 944 kg).

Accommodation: Normal flight crew of two and 15 passengers in individual seats on each side of central aisle. Optional 8-seat business executive transport arrangement. An 800-lb (363-kg) capacity ventral cargo pod (shown fitted above and on opposite page) may be carried.

Status: The prototype Model 99 was flown in July 1966 and the first production delivery followed on May 2, 1968, the 100th being delivered on April 28, 1969. The 36th production Model 99 served as a prototype for the Model 99A, deliveries of which began in 1969, and the 148th Model 99 series airliner delivered in November 1972 was the first to B99 standards. Approx. 160 Model 99s delivered by 1974.

Notes: Standard Model 99 has 550 shp PT6A-20 turboprops. Model B99 possesses similar power to that of Model 99A (see 1972 edition) but has a 500-lb (227-kg) increase in max. take-off weight, a new heavy-duty flap system and a new elevator system.

BEECHCRAFT B99

Dimensions: Span, 45 ft 10½ in (14,00 m); length, 44 ft 6¾ in (13,58 m); height, 14 ft 4⅓ in (4,40 m); wing area, 279·7 sq ft (25,985 m²).

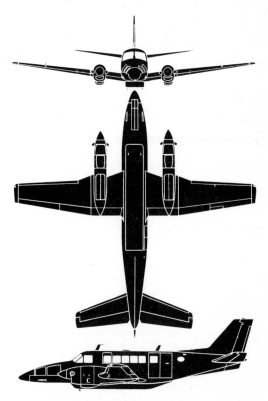

BEECHCRAFT SUPER KING AIR 200

Country of Origin: USA.

Type: Light business executive transport.

Power Plant: Two 850 shp Pratt & Whitney (UACL) PT6A-41 turboprops.

Performance: Max. cruise, 333 mph (536 km/h) at 12,000 ft (3 655 m), 320 mph (515 km/h) at 25,000 ft (7 620 m); max. range, 1,840 mls (2 961 km) at 27,000 ft (8 230 m) at max. cruise, 2,045 mls (3 290 km) at max. range cruise; initial climb, 2,520 ft/min (12,8 m/sec); service ceiling, 32,300 ft (9 845 m).

Weights: Empty equipped, 7,650 lb (3 470 kg); max. take-off, 12,500 lb (5 670 kg).

Accommodation: Flight crew of two and standard arrangement of six individual seats in main cabin with an optional eight-passenger arrangement. High-density configuration available.

Status: Prototype Super King Air flown October 27, 1972, with second example following on December 15. Customer deliveries were scheduled to commence February 1974.

Notes: The Super King Air 200 (also known as the Model 101) is the fourth aircraft in the King Air range and differs from the King Air A100 (see 1972 edition) primarily in having increased wing span, higher cabin pressure differential, increased fuel tankage, uprated turboprops and a T-tail arrangement. The King Air E90 (see 1973 edition) is basically a more powerful version of the C90 possessing similar turboprops to those of the A100. The C90, E90 and A100 remain in production, and deliveries of all King Air variants are expected to total 200 during 1974.

BEECHCRAFT SUPER KING AIR 200

Dimensions: Span, 54 ft 6 in (16,60 m); length, 43 ft 9 in (13,16 m); height, 14 ft 11$\frac{1}{2}$ in (4,54 m); wing area, 303 sq ft (28,1 m^2).

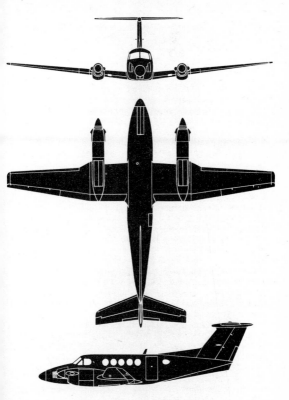

BOEING MODEL 727-200

Country of Origin: USA.

Type: Short- to medium-range commercial transport.

Power Plant: Three 14,500 lb (6 577 kg) Pratt & Whitney JT8D-9 turbofans (with 15,000 lb/6 804 kg JT8D-11s or 15,500 lb/7 030 kg JT8D-15s as options).

Performance: Max. speed, 621 mph (999 km/h) at 20,500 ft (6 250 m); max. cruise, 599 mph (964 km/h) at 24,700 ft (7 530 m); econ. cruise, 570 mph (917 km/h) at 30,000 ft (9 145 m); range with 26,400-lb (11 974-kg) payload and normal reserves, 2,850 mls (4 585 km), with max. payload (41,000 lb/18 597 kg), 1,845 mls (2 970 km); initial climb, 2,600 ft/min (13,2 m/sec).

Weights: Operational empty (basic), 97,525 lb (44 235 kg), (typical), 99,000 lb (44 905 kg); max. take-off, 208,000 lb (94 347 kg).

Accommodation: Crew of three on flight deck and six-abreast seating for 163 passengers in basic arrangement with max. seating for 189 passengers.

Status: First Model 727-100 flown February 9, 1963, with first delivery (to United) following October 29, 1963. Model 727-200 flown July 27, 1967, with first delivery (to Northeast) on December 11, 1967. Deliveries from mid-1972 have been of the so-called "Advanced 727-200" (to which specification refers and illustrations apply) and a total of approximately 1,100 Model 727s of all versions had been ordered by the beginning of 1974, of which 1,010 had been delivered.

Notes: The Model 727-200 is a "stretched" version of the 727-100 (see 1972 edition). Certification of the "Advanced 727" with JT8D-17 engines of 16,000 lb (7 257 kg) was scheduled for March 1974, permitting an increase of some 4,000 lb (1 815 kg) in payload.

BOEING MODEL 727-200

Dimensions: Span, 108 ft 0 in (32,92 m); length, 153 ft 2 in (46,69 m); height, 34 ft 0 in (10,36 m); wing area, 1,700 sq ft (157,9 m²).

BOEING MODEL 747B

Country of Origin: USA.
Type: Long-range large-capacity commercial transport.
Power Plant: Four 47,000 lb (21 320 kg) Pratt & Whitney JT9D-7W turbofans.
Performance: Max. speed at 600,000 lb (272 155 kg), 608 mph (978 km/h) at 30,000 ft (9 150 m); long-range cruise, 589 mph (948 km/h) at 35,000 ft (10 670 m); range with max. fuel and FAR reserves, 7,080 mls (11 395 km), with 79,618-lb (36 114-kg) payload, 6,620 mls (10 650 km); cruise ceiling, 45,000 ft (13 715 m).
Weights: Operational empty, 361,216 lb (163 844 kg); max. take-off, 775,000 lb (351 540 kg).
Accommodation: Normal flight crew of three and basic accommodation for 66 first-class and 308 economy-class passengers. Alternative layouts for 447 or 490 economy-class passengers nine- and 10-abreast respectively.
Status: First Model 747-100 flown on February 9, 1969, and first commercial services (by Pan American) inaugurated January 22, 1970. The first Model 747-200 (747B), the 88th aircraft off the assembly line, flown October 11, 1970.
Notes: Principal versions are the -100 and -200 series, the latter having greater fuel capacity and increased maximum take-off weight, convertible passenger/cargo and all-cargo versions of the -200 series (alias Model 747B) being designated 747C and 747F. The first production example of the latter flew on November 30, 1971. Deliveries of the Model 747SR, a short-range version of the 747-100 (to Japan Air Lines), began September 1973, in which month an order was placed (by Pan American) for the short-fuselage Model 747SP. The 747-300, flown on June 26, 1973, has 51,000 lb (23 133 kg) General Electric CF6-50D engines.

BOEING MODEL 747B

Dimensions: Span, 195 ft 8 in (59,64 m); length, 231 ft 4 in (70,51 m); height, 63 ft 5 in (19,33 m); wing area, 5,685 sq ft (528,15 m²).

BOEING EC-137D

Country of Origin: USA.

Type: Airborne warning and control system development aircraft.

Power Plant: Four 19,000 lb (8 618 kg) Pratt & Whitney JT3D-7 turbofans.

Performance: No details have been released for publication, but max. and econ. cruise speeds are likely to be generally similar to those of the equivalent commercial Model 707-320B (i.e., 627 mph/1 010 km/h and 550 mph/886 km/h respectively). Mission requirement is for 7-hr search at 29,000 ft (8 840 m) at 1,150 mls (1 850 km) from base.

Weights: Approx. max. take-off, 330,000 lb (149 685 kg).

Accommodation: The proposed production derivative, the E-3A, will carry an operational crew of 17 which may be increased according to mission.

Status: First of two EC-137D development aircraft flown February 9, 1972. At the beginning of 1974 it was proposed that three pre-production examples of the operational derivative, the E-3A, should be built (two possibly using the EC-137D airframes) with deliveries commencing in 1975. Subsequent production of 42 E-3As is envisaged.

Notes: As part of a programme for the development of a new AWACS (Airborne Warning And Control System) aircraft for operation by the USAF from the mid 'seventies, two Boeing 707-320B transports have been modified as EC-137D test-beds. These were employed during 1972 for competitive evaluation of the competing Hughes and Westinghouse radars, the latter having been selected as winning contender. The production E-3A, as planned at the beginning of 1974, will be powered by four 21,000 lb (9 525 kg) Pratt & Whitney TF33-P-7 turbofans with the possible alternative of a new 20,000–25,000 lb (9 072–11 340 kg) engine.

BOEING EC-137D

Dimensions: Span, 145 ft 9 in (44,42 m); length, 152 ft 11 in (46,61 m); height, 42 ft 5 in (12,93 m); wing area, 3,050 sq ft (283,4 m²).

BOEING T-43A

Country of Origin: USA.

Type: Military navigational trainer.

Power Plant: Two 14,500 lb (6 577 kg) Pratt & Whitney JT8D-9 turbofans.

Performance: Max. speed, 576 mph (927 km/h) at 23,000 ft (7 010 m); max. range, 3,225 mls (5 190 km); training mission endurance, 1 hr 30 min at low altitude, 4 hr 40 min at long-range cruise at 35,000 ft (10 668 m), 5 hr 30 min at max. time cruise at 30,000 ft (9 144 m).

Weights: Zero fuel, 68,454 lb (31 050 kg); design mission gross, 106,167 lb (48 157 kg); max. take-off, 115,500 lb (52 390 kg).

Accommodation: Flight crew of two. Cabin provides three instructor stations, 12 student stations and four navigator proficiency stations.

Status: First of 19 T-43As ordered by USAF flown on April 10, 1973, with completion of deliveries scheduled for July 1974.

Notes: Ordered in May 1971 as a successor to the piston-engined Convair T-29 at the USAF Air Training Command's Navigation Training School at Mather, the T-43A is basically a modified Model 737-200 commercial transport (see 1973 edition) airframe with several new features specified by the USAF, including an aft body fuselage fuel tank in the space normally occupied by the rear underfloor baggage hold and provision for a further fuselage tank. The T-43A incorporates all the improvements that have been engineered for the so-called "Advanced 737-200", which standard was introduced from May 1971. A total of 360 examples of the commercial transport had been ordered by November 1973.

BOEING T-43A

Dimensions: Span, 93 ft 0 in (28,35 m); length, 100 ft 0 in (30,48 m); height, 37 ft 0 in (11,28 m); wing area, 980 sq ft (91,05 m²).

BRITTEN-NORMAN BN-2A ISLANDER

Country of Origin: United Kingdom.
Type: Light utility transport.
Power Plant: Two 260 hp Lycoming O-540-E4C5 six-cylinder horizontally-opposed engines.
Performance: Max. speed, 170 mph (273 km/h) at sea level; cruise at 75% power, 160 mph (257 km/h) at 7,000 ft (2 140 m), at 67% power, 158 mph (253 km/h) at 9,000 ft (2 750 m), at 59% power, 154 mph (248 km/h) at 13,000 ft (3 960 m); range with standard fuel, 717 mls (1 154 km) at 160 mph (257 km/h), 870 mls (1 400 km) at 154 mph (248 km/h), tip tanks, 1,040 mls (1 674 km) at 160 mph (257 km/h), 1,263 mls (2 035 km) at 154 mph (248 km/h).
Weights: Empty equipped, 3,675 lb (1 667 kg); max. take-off, 6,600 lb (2 993 kg).
Accommodation: Flight crew of one or two and up to 10 passengers on pairs of bench-type seats.
Status: Prototype flown June 12, 1965, followed by first production aircraft on August 20, 1966. More than 450 ordered by beginning of 1974. Production transferred to Fairey SA in Belgium during 1973, the first Belgian-built example delivered in December of that year, and 215 airframes being manufactured under contract by IRMA in Rumania.
Notes: The BN-2A-8S illustrated on opposite page, and to which the above specification applies, is the latest development in the Islander series, and was first flown on August 22, 1972. By comparison with the BN-2A-8 (illustrated above), it features a 45·5-in (1,15-m) longer nose to provide increased baggage space, an additional cabin window each side at the rear, and provision for an additional seat row. These changes, indicated by the suffix "S" (for Stretched), are being offered as customer options.

BRITTEN-NORMAN BN-2A ISLANDER

Dimensions: Span, 49 ft 0 in (14,94 m); length, 39 ft 5¼ in (12,02 m); height, 13 ft 8 in (4,16 m); wing area, 325 sq ft (30,2 m²).

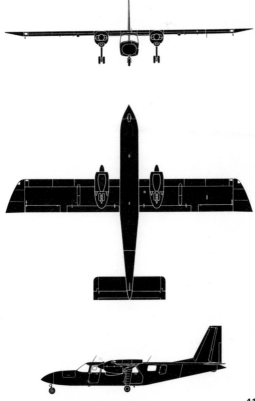

BRITTEN-NORMAN BN-2A MK III
TRISLANDER

Country of Origin: United Kingdom.

Type: Light utility transport and feederliner.

Power Plant: Three 260 hp Lycoming O-540-E4C5 six-cylinder horizontally-opposed engines.

Performance: Max. speed, 183 mph (294 km/h) at sea level; cruise at 75% power, 176 mph (283 km/h) at 6,500 ft (1 980 m), at 67% power, 175 mph (282 km/h) at 9,000 ft (2 750 m); range with max. payload, 160 mls (257 km) at 170 mph (274 km/h), with 2,400-lb (1 089-kg) payload, 700 mls (1 127 km) at 175 mph (282 km/h).

Weights: Empty equipped, 5,700 lb (2 585 kg); max. take-off, 10,000 lb (4 536 kg).

Accommodation: Flight crew of one or two, and 16–17 passengers in pairs on bench-type seats.

Status: Prototype flown September 11, 1970, with production prototype flying on March 6, 1971. First production Trislander flown April 29, 1971, and first delivery (to Aurigny) following on June 29, 1971. Trislander production was transferred to Fairey SA at Gosselies, Belgium, late in 1972, and deliveries from the new line were expected early 1974 with production of 30 scheduled for the 1974–75 financial year, three per month being delivered from September 1974.

Notes: The Trislander is a derivative of the Islander (see pages 40–41) with which it has 75% commonality. The wingtip auxiliary fuel tanks optional on the Islander have been standardised for the Trislander, and the only significant differences between the two aircraft are the extra 7 ft 6 in (2,29 m) section ahead of the wing and the strengthened fin structure carrying the third engine.

BRITTEN-NORMAN BN-2A MK III TRISLANDER

Dimensions: Span, 53 ft 0 in (16,15 m); length, 43 ft 9 in (13,33 m); height, 14 ft 2 in (4,32 m); wing area, 337 sq ft (31,25 m²).

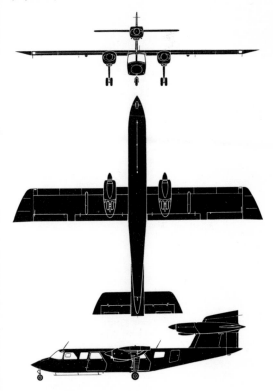

CASA C.212 AVIOCAR

Country of Origin: Spain.
Type: STOL utility transport, navigational trainer and photographic survey aircraft.
Power Plant: Two 776 eshp (715 shp) Garrett-AiResearch TPE 331-5-251C turboprops.
Performance: (At 13,889 lb/6 300 kg) Max. cruise, 243 mph (391 km/h) at 12,000 ft (3 658 m), 238 mph (383 km/h) at 5,000 ft (1 524 m); initial climb, 1,724 ft/min (8,76 m/sec); service ceiling, 24,605 ft (7 500 m); range with max. payload and reserves (30 min hold at 5,000 ft/ 1 524 m plus 5% take-off weight), 205 mls (330 km) at 12,500 ft (3 810 m), with max. fuel and similar reserves, 1,197 mls (1 927 km).
Weights: Empty equipped, 8,045 lb (3 650 kg); max. take-off, 13,889 lb (6 300 kg); max. payload, 4,409 lb (2 000 kg).
Accommodation: Flight crew of two and 18 passengers in commercial configuration. Ten casualty stretchers and three sitting casualties or medical attendants in ambulance configuration. Provision for up to 15 paratroops and jumpmaster or 4,409 lb (2 000 kg) of cargo.
Status: Two prototypes flown March 26 and October 23, 1971, with first of 12 pre-production examples following November 17, 1972. Initial production batch of 32 for Spanish Air Force with deliveries commencing early 1974.
Notes: Of pre-production series, eight will be delivered to Air Force (six for photo survey and two as navigational trainers), and of initial production batch 29 will be cargo-paratroop transports and three will be navigational trainers.

CASA C.212 AVIOCAR

Dimensions: Span, 62 ft 4 in (19,00 m); length, 49 ft 10½ in (15,20 m); height, 20 ft 8¾ in (6,32 m); wing area, 430·556 sq ft (40,0 m²).

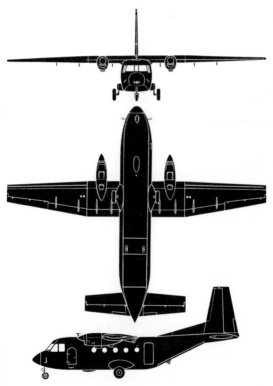

CESSNA T337G
PRESSURISED SKYMASTER

Country of Origin: USA.

Type: Light cabin monoplane.

Power Plant: Two 225 hp Teledyne Continental TSIO-360-C six-cylinder horizontally-opposed engines.

Performance: Max. speed, 250 mph (402 km/h) at 20,000 ft (6 096 m); cruise at 75% power, 228 mph (367 km/h) at 16,000 ft (4 877 m), at 65% power, 221 mph (356 km/h) at 20,000 ft (6 096 m); max. range, 1,325 mls (2 132 km) at 20,000 ft (6 096 m), 1,505 mls (2 422 km) at 16,000 ft (4 877 m); initial climb, 1,250 ft/min (6,3 m/sec).

Weights: Empty equipped, 2,900 lb (1 315 kg); max. take-off, 4,700 lb (2 132 kg).

Accommodation: Pilot and co-pilot or passenger seated side-by-side with dual controls and rear seat for two or three passengers.

Status: Derived from the non-pressurised Model 337 Skymaster, the T337G was first flown in 1971, customer deliveries commencing August 1972. Licence production of the T337G initiated in France by Reims Aviation during 1973.

Notes: The T337G differs from earlier production models of the Skymaster in introducing a pressure shell between the two engine firewalls and a revised cabin window arrangement. It replaces the non-pressurised T337F Turbo Super Skymaster in the Cessna range. The Model 337 was introduced in February 1965, and some 1,500 aircraft of this basic type had been delivered by the beginning of 1973, plus 510 examples of two military versions, the O-2A equipped for the forward air control mission and the O-2B equipped for psychological warfare missions.

46

CESSNA T337G PRESSURISED SKYMASTER

Dimensions: Span, 38 ft 2 in (11,63 m); length, 29 ft 9 in (9,07 m); height, 9 ft 4 in (2,84 m); wing area, 202·5 sq ft (18,81 m²).

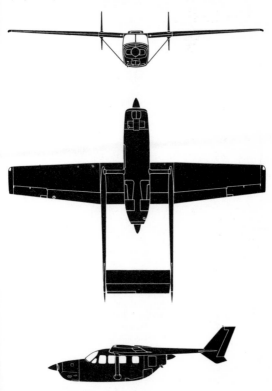

CESSNA MODEL 340

Country of Origin: USA.

Type: Light business executive transport.

Power Plant: Two 285 hp Teledyne Continental TSIO-520-K six-cylinder horizontally-opposed engines.

Performance: Max. speed, 221 mph (356 km/h) at sea level, 260 mph (418 km/h) at 16,000 ft (4 877 m); max. cruise, 219 mph (352 km/h) at 10,000 ft (3 048 m), 241 mph (388 km/h) at 20,000 ft (6 096 m); range (no reserves), 663 mls (1 067 km) at 215 mph (346 km/h) at 10,000 ft (3 048 m), 726 mls (1 168 km) at 20,000 ft (6 096 m) at 236 mph (380 km/h), (max. auxiliary fuel), 1,475 mls (2 373 km) at 20,000 ft (6 096 m); initial climb, 1,500 ft/min (7,62 m/sec); service ceiling, 26,500 ft (8 077 m).

Weights: Empty equipped, 3,723 lb (1 689 kg); max. take-off, 5,975 lb (2 710 kg).

Accommodation: Standard seating for pilot and co-pilot forward with individual seats for four passengers.

Status: Development of the Model 340 was initiated in 1969, but the first prototype was lost in the spring of 1970. Production deliveries commenced early 1972.

Notes: The first pressurised aircraft in the light-twin category at the time of its introduction, the Model 340 was evolved from the non-pressurised Model 310, introducing a new pressurised capsule-type fuselage of fail-safe design, and wings and undercarriage generally similar to those of the larger and more powerful Model 414. Production of Models 310 and 414 continued in parallel with the Model 340 during 1973, together with the externally-similar Models 402 (see 1970 edition) and 421B Golden Eagle (see 1971 edition).

CESSNA MODEL 340

Dimensions: Span, 38 ft 1½ in (11,62 m); length, 34 ft 4 in (10,46 m); height, 12 ft 6⅔ in (3,83 m); wing area, 184·7 sq ft (17,16 m²).

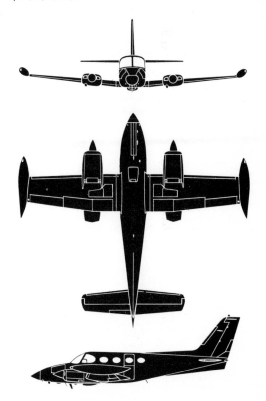

CESSNA CITATION SERIES 500

Country of Origin: USA.

Type: Light business executive transport.

Power Plant: Two 2,200 lb (1 000 kg) Pratt & Whitney JT15D-1 turbofans.

Performance: Max. speed, 402 mph (647 km/h) at 26,400 ft (8 046 m); max. cruise, 400 mph (644 km/h) at 25,400 ft (7 740 m); range with eight persons and 45 min reserves at 90% cruise thrust, 1,397 mls (2 248 km), with two persons and same reserves at 90% cruise thrust, 1,502 mls (2 417 km); initial climb, 2,900 ft/min (14,7 m/sec); service ceiling, 38,400 ft (11 704 m).

Weights: Empty 6,390 lb (2 898 kg); max. take-off, 11,500 lb (5 217 kg).

Accommodation: Crew of two on separate flight deck and alternative arrangements for five or six passengers in main cabin.

Status: First of two prototypes flown on September 15, 1969, and first production Citation flown in May 1971. Customer deliveries began in October 1971 with 80 having been scheduled for delivery during 1973 when production was to have attained 10 per month by year's end, with 120 scheduled for delivery during course of 1974.

Notes: The Citation places emphasis on short-field performance, balanced field length being 2,950 ft (899 m) and take-off distance to clear a 35-ft (10,7-m) obstacle being 2,300 ft (701 m), enabling the aircraft to use some 2,300 US airfields. The current Citation Series 500 was to have been supplemented from 1977 by a more advanced light business executive transport referred to as the "Series 600", but development of this type was deferred late 1973.

CESSNA CITATION SERIES 500

Dimensions: Span, 43 ft 8½ in (13,32 m); length, 43 ft 6 in (13,26 m); height, 14 ft 3¾ in (4,36 m); wing area, 260 sq ft (24,15 m²).

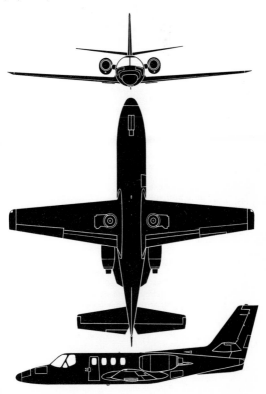

CESSNA A-37B DRAGONFLY

Country of Origin: USA.
Type: Two-seat light tactical strike aircraft.
Power Plant: Two 2,850 lb (1 293 kg) General Electric J85-GE-17A turbojets.
Performance: Max. speed, 507 mph (816 km/h) at 16,000 ft (4 875 m); max. cruise, 489 mph (787 km/h) at 25,000 ft (7 620 m); range (with max. external fuel), 1,012 mls (1 628 km), (with max. ordnance), 460 mls (740 km); initial climb, 6,990 ft/min (35,1 m/sec); service ceiling, 41,765 ft (12 730 m).
Weights: Empty equipped, 6,211 lb (2 817 kg); max. take-off, 14,000 lb (6 350 kg).
Armament: One 7,62-mm GAU-2B/A Minigun in forward fuselage and provision for up to 4,100 lb (1 860 kg) of ordnance on eight wing stations, the four inboard stations being of 870 lb (394 kg) capacity, the two intermediate stations being of 600 lb (272 kg) and the two outer stations having 500 lb (227 kg) capacity.
Status: Prototype A-37B flown September 1967, being preceded by 39 A-37As (converted from T-37B trainer airframes). Production deliveries of the A-37B, initiated in 1968, were continuing at the beginning of 1974 when some 450 examples had been manufactured.
Notes: The A-37B is a light strike derivative of the T-37 basic trainer with J85 turbojets supplanting 1,025 lb (465 kg) Continental T69-T-25s, some structural strengthening and redesign and provision for a variety of external ordnance loads. The A-37B equips three Tactical Fighter Groups of the US Air National Guard, has been supplied to the Vietnamese Air Force and was being delivered to the air forces of Peru (24) and Khmer (24) in 1974.

CESSNA A-37B DRAGONFLY

Dimensions: Span (over tip tanks), 35 ft $10\frac{1}{2}$ in (10,93 m); length, 29 ft $3\frac{1}{2}$ in (8,93 m); height, 8 ft $10\frac{1}{2}$ in (2,70 m); wing area, 183·9 sq ft (17,09 m^2).

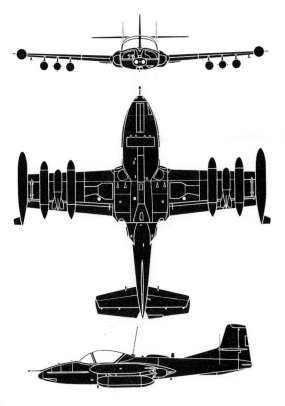

DASSAULT-BREGUET FALCON 10

Country of Origin: France.

Type: Light business executive transport.

Power Plant: Two 3,230 lb (1 465 kg) Garrett-AiResearch TFE-731-2 turbofans.

Performance: Max. cruise, 567 mph (912 km/h) at 30,000 ft (9 145 m), 495 mph (796 km/h) or Mach 0·75 at 45,000 ft (13 716 m); range with four passengers and 45 min reserves, 2,070 mls (3 330 km) at 45,000 ft (13 716 m), 1,495 mls (2 405 km) at max. cruise at 30,000 ft (9 145 m).

Weights: Empty equipped, 10,417 lb (4 725 kg); max. take-off, 18,298 lb (8 300 kg).

Accommodation: Flight crew of two with provision for third crew member on jump seat. Executive version for four passengers with alternative arrangement for seven passengers.

Status: First of three prototypes flown December 1, 1970, followed by second on October 15, 1971, and third on October 16, 1972. The first production Falcon10 was flown on April 30, 1973, and production deliveries began during November of that year, output being two per month at the beginning of 1974.

Notes: The Falcon 10 (also known as the Mystère 10) is basically a scaled-down version of the Falcon 20, and at a later stage in development it is proposed to offer the 2,980 lb (1 350 kg) Turboméca-SNECMA Larzac turbofan as an alternative power plant, the second prototype commencing trials during 1973 with a Larzac in its starboard engine nacelle. The Falcon 10 is being offered to the *Armée de l'Air* as a military crew trainer and liaison aircraft, and two examples have been ordered for test and evaluation purposes.

DASSAULT-BREGUET FALCON 10

Dimensions: 42 ft 11 in (13,08 m); length, 45 ft 5¾ in (13,86 m); height, 14 ft 5⅔ in (4,41 m); wing area, 259·4 sq ft (24,1 m²).

DASSAULT-BREGUET FALCON 20

Country of Origin: France.

Type: Light business executive transport.

Power Plant: Two 4,315 lb (1 983 kg) General Electric CF700-2D-2 turbofans.

Performance: Max. speed, 404 mph (650 km/h) at sea level, 449 mph (722 km/h) at 22,965 ft (7 000 m); max. cruise at 20,000 lb (9 072 kg), 535 mph (860 km/h) at 25,000 ft (7 620 m); econ. cruise, 466 mph (750 km/h) at 40,000 ft (12 190 m); range with eight passengers and 45 min reserves, 2,300 mls (3 580 km) at 39,370 ft (12 000 m); max. operating altitude, 42,650 ft (13 000 m).

Weights: Empty equipped, 15,972 lb (7 245 kg); max. take-off, 28,660 lb (13 000 kg).

Accommodation: Normal flight crew of two and standard arrangement for eight passengers in individual seats. Alternative arrangements available for from 10 to 14 passengers.

Status: First Falcon 20 (also known as the Mystère 20) flown May 4, 1963, followed by first production aircraft on January 1, 1965. Current models are the Series E and Series F, these being similar apart from wing high-lift devices.

Notes: In continuous production for ten years, the Falcon 20 in its Series E and F versions differs from the Series D which they have supplanted in having slight increases in fuel capacity and range, improved electrical systems and a higher take-off weight. The Series F differs from the Series E in having a leading-edge slat inboard of each wing fence, a slotted leading-edge slat outboard of each fence, and slightly modified trailing-edge flaps. A military systems training version is known as the Falcon ST.

DASSAULT-BREGUET FALCON 20

Dimensions: Span, 53 ft 6 in (16,30 m); length, 56 ft 3 in (17,15 m); height, 17 ft 5 in (5,32 m); wing area, 440 sq ft (41,0 m²).

DASSAULT-BREGUET FALCON 30

Country of Origin: France.
Type: Third-level airliner.
Power Plant: Two 6,063 lb (2 750 kg) Avco-Lycoming ALF-502D turbofans.
Performance: (Estimated) Max. cruise, 509 mph (820 km/h) at 25,000 ft (7 620 m); econ. cruise, 441 mph (710 km/h) at 35,000 ft (10 670 m); range with max. payload (7,495 lb/3 400 kg), 870 mls (1 400 km).
Weights: Empty equipped, 21,825 lb (9 900 kg); max. take-off, 35,275 lb (16 000 kg).
Accommodation: Normal flight crew of two and standard accommodation for 30 passengers in three-abreast seating.
Status: First of two prototypes flown May 11, 1973, with second (definitive) prototype scheduled to fly mid-1974, production deliveries being planned for early 1976.
Notes: The Falcon 30 (alias Mystère 30) has been evolved via an earlier project (Falcon 20-T) which was to have featured a smaller diameter fuselage utilised by the first prototype (illustrated above). The second or definitive prototype will feature the larger-diameter fuselage (illustrated on opposite page). A three-engined derivative, the Falcon 30T, exists as a long-term project and another projected variant is the high-density Falcon 40 with accommodation for up to 40 passengers in four-abreast seating.

DASSAULT-BREGUET FALCON 30

Dimensions: Span, 59 ft 1$\frac{1}{2}$ in (18,03 m); length, 64 ft 11 in (19,77 m); height, 19 ft 10 in (6,05 m); wing area, 530 sq ft (49,0 m^2).

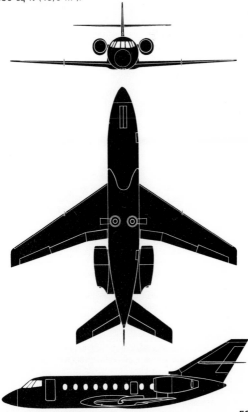

DASSAULT-BREGUET MERCURE 100

Country of Origin: France.
Type: Short-range commercial transport.
Power Plant: Two 15,500 lb (7 030 kg) Pratt & Whitney JT8D-15 turbofans.
Performance: Max. cruise, 579 mph (932 km/h) at 20,000 ft (6 100 m); econ. cruise, 533 mph (858 km/h) at 30,000 ft (9 145 m); range cruise, 512 mph (825 km/h) at 35,100 ft (10 700 m); range with max. payload (35,274 lb/16 000 kg), 466 mls (750 km) at max. cruise at 25,000 ft (7 620 m), with max. fuel and 28,420-lb (12 790-kg) payload, 1,025 mls (1 650 km); max. sea level climb at 100,000 lb (45 359 kg), 3,300 ft/min (16,76 m/sec).
Weights: Operational empty, 68,563 lb (31 100 kg); max. take-off, 119,227 lb (54 500 kg).
Accommodation: Normal flight crew of two and typical mixed-class accommodation for 132 passengers (12 first-class passengers in four-abreast seating and 120 tourist-class passengers in six-abreast seating), or alternative single-class arrangements for 140 and 150 passengers in six-abreast seating throughout.
Status: Two prototypes flown May 28, 1971, and September 7, 1972, respectively, with first production aircraft following on July 17, 1973, with delivery (to Air Inter) scheduled for April 1974 with a further four following during the course of the year
Notes: The production Mercure, 2·75 ft (84 cm) longer than the prototype aircraft, is expected to receive certification in April 1974, and is being manufactured in co-operation with Aeritalia (Italy), CASA (Spain), SABCA (Belgium), F + W (Switzerland) and Canadair (Canada), all of which have contributed towards the launching programme.

DASSAULT-BREGUET MERCURE 100

Dimensions: Span, 100 ft 3 in (30,55 m); length, 114 ft 3$\frac{2}{3}$ in (34,84 m); height, 37 ft 3$\frac{1}{4}$ in (11,36 m); wing area, 1,248·6 sq ft (116,0 m²).

DASSAULT-BREGUET MIRAGE 5

Country of Origin: France.

Type: Single-seat ground attack fighter.

Power Plant: One 9,436 lb (4 280 kg) dry and 13,670 lb (6 200 kg) reheat SNECMA Atar 9C turbojet.

Performance: Max. speed (clean), 835 mph (1 335 km/h) or Mach 1·1 at sea level, 1,386 mph (2 230 km/h) or Mach 2·1 at 39,370 ft (12 000 m); cruise, 594 mph (956 km/h) at 36,090 ft (11 000 m); combat radius with 2,000-lb (907-kg) bomb load (hi-lo-hi profile), 805 mls (1 300 km), (lo-lo-lo profile), 400 mls (650 km); time to 36,090 ft (11 000 m) at Mach 0·9, 3 min, to 49,210 ft (15 000 m) at Mach 1·8, 6 min 50 sec.

Weights: Empty equipped, 14,550 lb (6 600 kg); max. loaded, 29,760 lb (13 500 kg).

Armament: Two 30-mm DEFA 5-52 cannon with 125 rpg and seven external ordnance stations. Maximum external load (ordnance and fuel), 9,260 lb (4 200 kg).

Status: Prototype flown May 19, 1967, and first deliveries (to Peru) following May 1968. Assembly (for Belgian Air Force) completed in Belgium by SABCA late 1972. Deliveries to Libya, Abu Dhabi, Pakistan and Peru continuing in 1974.

Notes: The Mirage 5 is an export version of the Mirage IIIE (see 1967 edition) optimised for the ground attack role and featuring simplified avionics. Orders fulfilled or in process of fulfilment at beginning of 1974 included 30 (including two two-seaters) for Pakistan, 24 for Peru (including two two-seaters), 14 for Colombia (plus four two-seat Mirage IIIs), 106 for Belgium (including 16 two-seaters and 63 for tac-recce role), 110 for Libya (including 10 two-seaters), six for Venezuela (including two two-seaters), 14 for Abu Dhabi (including two two-seaters), and 50 for the *Armée de l'Air*. The two-seat Mirage 5B offers tandem seating and is intended primarily for the training role.

DASSAULT-BREGUET MIRAGE 5

Dimensions: Span, 26 ft $11\frac{1}{2}$ in (8,22 m); length, 51 ft $0\frac{1}{4}$ in (15,55 m); height, 13 ft $11\frac{1}{2}$ in (4,25 m); wing area, 375·12 sq ft (34,85 m²).

DASSAULT-BREGUET MIRAGE F1

Country of Origin: France.

Type: Single-seat multi-purpose fighter.

Power Plant: One 11,023 lb (5 000 kg) dry and 15,873 lb (7 200 kg) reheat SNECMA Atar 9K-50 turbojet.

Performance: Max. speed (clean), 915 mph (1 472 km/h) or Mach 1·2 at sea level, 1,450 mph (2 335 km/h) or Mach 2·2 at 39,370 ft (12 000 m); range cruise, 550 mph (885 km/h) at 29,530 ft (9 000 m); range with max. external fuel, 2,050 mls (3 300 km), with max. external combat load of 8,818 lb (4 000 kg), 560 mls (900 km), with external combat load of 4,410 lb (2 000 kg), 1,430 mls (2 300 km); service ceiling, 65,600 ft (20 000 m).

Weights: Empty, 16,314 lb (7 400 kg); loaded (clean), 24,030 lb (10 900 kg); max. take-off, 32,850 lb (14 900 kg).

Armament: Two 30-mm DEFA cannon and (intercept) 1-3 Matra 530 Magic and two AIM-9 Sidewinder AAMs.

Status: First of four prototypes flown December 23, 1966. First of 105 ordered for *Armée de l'Air* flown February 15, 1973. Production rate of three per month at beginning of 1974. Licence manufacture is to be undertaken in South Africa with deliveries commencing 1977.

Notes: Initial model for *Armée de l'Air* intended primarily for high-altitude intercept role. Proposed versions include F1A for day ground attack role, the F1B two-seat trainer, the F1C interceptor, the F1E M53-powered multi-role version, and the F1R reconnaissance model. Fifteen Mirage F1s have been ordered by Spain (which country has an option on 18 more) and delivery of 16 Mirage F1CZ interceptors to South Africa will commence during 1974, these being followed by 32 Mirage F1AZ ground attack fighters. The F1E will have the M53 engine of 12,345 lb (5 600 kg) and 18,740 lb (8 500 kg) with reheat.

DASSAULT-BREGUET MIRAGE F1

Dimensions: Span, 27 ft 6¾ in (8,40 m); length, 49 ft 2½ in (15,00 m); height, 14 ft 9 in (4,50 m); wing area, 269·098 sq ft (25 m²).

DASSAULT-BREGUET SUPER ÉTENDARD

Country of Origin: France.
Type: Single-seat shipboard strike fighter.
Power Plant: One 10,912 lb (4 950 kg) SNECMA Atar 8K-50 turbojet.
Performance: (Estimated) Max. speed (clean), 695 mph (1 118 km/h) or Mach 1·05 at 36,000 ft (11 000 m), 708 mph (1 139 km/h) or Mach 0·93 at sea level; tactical radius (internal fuel), 210 mls (338 km) at sea level, 520 mls (837 km) at 42,650 ft (13 000 m); initial climb, 20,000 ft/min (101,6 m/sec).
Weights: (Estimated) Empty equipped, 14,000 lb (6 350 kg); max. take-off, 24,500 lb (11 113 kg).
Armament: Two 30-mm DEFA cannon in forward fuselage and five external stores stations (one under fuselage and four under wings) for up to approximately 4,000 lb (1 815 kg) of ordnance.
Status: Super Étendard prototype (modified Étendard IVM airframe) scheduled to commence test programme before end of 1974 following re-engined Étendard IVM with Atar 8K-50 to fly second quarter of 1974. One hundred Super Étendards ordered August 1973 for *Aéronavale* with deliveries to commence 1976.
Notes: More powerful derivative of Étendard IVM (see 1965 edition) with new avionics and some 90 per cent identical structure to that of earlier aircraft.

DASSAULT-BREGUET SUPER ÉTENDARD

Dimensions: Span, 31 ft 6 in (9,60 m); length, 47 ft 3 in (14,40 m); height, 14 ft 2 in (4,30 m); wing area, 312 sq ft (29,0 m²).

DASSAULT-BREGUET/DORNIER
ALPHA JET

Countries of Origin: France and Federal Germany.

Type: Two-seat light tactical aircraft and advanced trainer.

Power Plant: Two 2,960 lb (1 345 kg) SNECMA/Turbo-méca Larzac 04 turbofans.

Performance: (Estimated) Max. speed (clean), 575 mph (925 km/h) at sea level, 580 mph (933 km/h) at 36,090 ft (11 000 m); max. range (with external fuel), 1,243 mls (2 000 km) at 485 mph (780 km/h); max. endurance, 2 hr 35 min; typical endurance (low-level training mission without external fuel), 1 hr 40 min; service ceiling, 45,930 ft (14 000 m).

Weights: Empty equipped, 6,945–7,275 lb (3 150–3 300 kg); normal loaded (trainer), 9,744 lb (4 420 kg); max. take-off (trainer), 10,542 lb (4 782 kg), (strike), 15,430 lb (7 000 kg).

Armament: (Strike) One 30-mm DEFA cannon with 150 rounds beneath fuselage and four underwing stores stations each capable of carrying one 250-lb (113,4-kg), 500-lb (226,8-kg) or 1,000-lb (453,6-kg) bomb, a 600-lb (272-kg) cluster dispenser or a pod containing 36 2·75-in (7-cm) rockets.

Status: First of four prototypes was flown at Istres on October 26, 1973, with the remaining three having been scheduled to follow in January, May and October 1974.

Planned production of some 400 for *Armée de l'Air* and *Luftwaffe* with deliveries commencing October 1976 from two final assembly lines (Toulouse and Munich).

Notes: Alpha Jet to be used for basic and advanced training by the *Armée de l'Air* and for ground attack by the *Luftwaffe* (latter version illustrated on opposite page). Thirty-three have been ordered for the training role by Belgium.

DASSAULT-BREGUET/DORNIER ALPHA JET

Dimensions: Span, 30 ft 0½ in (9,16 m); length, 38 ft 7 in (11,70 m); height, 13 ft 7 in (4,15 m); wing area, 188·4 sq ft (17,5 m²).

DE HAVILLAND CANADA DHC-6
TWIN OTTER SERIES 300

Country of Origin: Canada.

Type: STOL utility transport and feederliner.

Power Plant: Two 652 eshp Pratt & Whitney PT6A-27 turboprops.

Performance: Max. cruise, 210 mph (338 km/h) at 10,000 ft (3 050 m); range at max. cruise with 3,250-lb (1 474-kg) payload, 745 mls (1 198 km), with 14 passengers and 45 min reserves, 780 mls (1 255 km); initial climb at 12,500 lb (5 670 kg), 1,600 ft/min (8,1 m/sec); service ceiling, 26,700 ft (8 138 m).

Weights: Basic operational (including pilot), 7,000 lb (3 180 kg); max. take-off, 12,500 lb (5 670 kg).

Accommodation: Flight crew of one or two and accommodation for up to 20 passengers in basic commuter arrangement. Optional commuter layouts for 18 or 19 passengers, and 13–20-passenger utility version.

Status: First of five (Series 100) pre-production aircraft flown May 20, 1965. Series 100 superseded by Series 200 (see 1969 edition) in April 1968, the latter being joined by the Series 300 with the 231st aircraft off the assembly line, deliveries of this version commencing spring 1969. Total ordered by beginning of 1974 in excess of 380 when production was continuing at six per month.

Notes: Series 100 and 200 Twin Otters feature a shorter nose and have 579 eshp PT6A-20s, and the Twin Otter is available as a floatplane. The series 300S introduced in 1973 features upper wing spoilers, high-capacity brakes, an anti-skid braking system and other improvements.

DHC-6 TWIN OTTER SERIES 300

Dimensions: Span, 65 ft 0 in (19,81 m); length, 51 ft 9 in (15,77 m); height, 18 ft 7 in (5,66 m); wing area, 420 sq ft (39,02 m²).

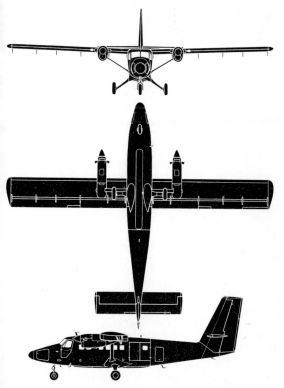

DE HAVILLAND CANADA DHC-7 DASH-7

Country of Origin: Canada.
Type: STOL short-haul commercial transport.
Power Plant: Four 1,120 shp Pratt & Whitney (UACL) PT6A-50 turboprops.
Performance: (Estimated) Max. cruise, 274 mph (441 km/h) at 7,500 ft (2 286 m); long-range cruise, 230 mph (370 km/h) at 20,000 ft (6 096 m); range with max. payload (11,060 lb/5 017 kg), 733 mls (1 180 km), with max. fuel, 2,003 mls (3 223 km).
Weights: Operational empty, 24,440 lb (11 130 kg); max. take-off, 41,000 lb (18 597 kg).
Accommodation: Flight crew of two and basic accommodation for 48 passengers with optional arrangement for 54 passengers.
Status: First of two pre-production aircraft scheduled to commence flight test programme late in 1974 with current planning calling for the first production aircraft to be flown in June 1975.
Notes: The result of a world-wide market survey of short-haul transport requirements, the DHC-7 STOL (short take-off and landing) airliner is being jointly funded by de Havilland Canada, United Aircraft (manufacturers of the engines) and the Canadian Government, and the US Boeing concern is expected to provide marketing support. The aircraft has been designed to operate with a full load of passengers from 2,000-ft (610-m) runways and will feature a quiet engine/propeller combination which will limit external noise during take-off and landing. The two pre-production examples of the DHC-7 are being built on production tooling and will be fully representative of the production standard, and an initial two-per-month production rate is anticipated which could be expanded to four aircraft per month by 1977.

DE HAVILLAND CANADA DHC-7 DASH-7

Dimensions: Span, 93 ft 0 in (28,35 m); length, 80 ft 4 in (24,50 m); height, 26 ft 3 in (8,00 m); wing area, 860 sq ft (79,9 m²).

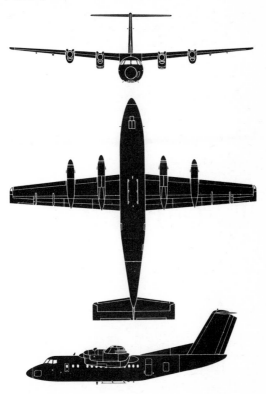

DORNIER DO 28D-2 SKYSERVANT

Country of Origin: Federal Germany.

Type: Light STOL utility aircraft.

Power Plant: Two 380 hp Lycoming IGSO-540-A1E six-cylinder horizontally-opposed engines.

Performance: Max. speed, 199 mph (320 km/h) at 10,000 ft (3 050 m); max. cruise at 75% power, 178 mph (286 km/h) at 10,000 ft (3 050 m); econ. cruise, 143 mph (230 km/h); range with max. fuel and without reserves at econ. cruise, 1,143 mls (1 837 km); initial climb, 1,180 ft/min (6 m/sec); service ceiling, 24,280 ft (7 400 m).

Weights: Empty, 4,775 lb (2 166 kg); max. take-off, 8,378 lb (3 800 kg).

Accommodation: Flight crew of one or two, and 12 passengers in individual seats in main cabin, 13 passengers in inward-facing folding seats, or (ambulance role) five casualty stretchers and five seats for attendants or casualties.

Status: First of three prototype Do 28Ds flown February 23, 1966, with production deliveries commencing summer 1967. Total of more than 200 Do 28Ds delivered by beginning of 1974 when production rate was six—eight per month.

Notes: Total of 125 Do 28Ds have been delivered to *Luftwaffe* (105) and *Marineflieger* (20), four of those for the former service are used by the VIP transport unit, the *Flugbereitschaft*. The Skyservant may be fitted with wheel-ski gear or floats, and from the beginning of 1973 production has concentrated on the D-2 version with increased fuel capacity and maximum take-off weight, a 6-in (15-cm) increase in cabin length and improved flaps and ailerons.

DORNIER DO 28D-2 SKYSERVANT

Dimensions: Span, 50 ft 10¾ in (15,50 m); length, 37 ft 4¾ in (11,40 m); height, 12 ft 9½ in (3,90 m); wing area, 308 sq ft (28,6 m²).

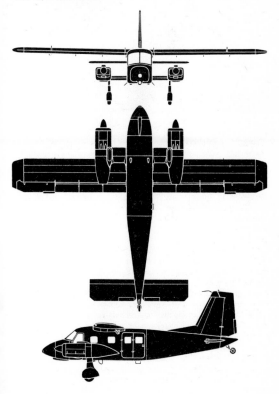

EMBRAER EMB-110 BANDEIRANTE

Country of Origin: Brazil.
Type: Light general-purpose and utility aircraft.
Power Plant: Two 680 shp Pratt & Whitney (UACL) PT6A-27 turboprops.
Performance: Max. cruise, 260 mph (418 km/h) at 9,840 ft (3 000 m); max. range (with 30 min reserves), 1,150 mls (1 850 km); initial climb, 1,968 ft/min (10 m/sec); service ceiling (at 10,692 lb/4 850 kg), 27,950 ft (8 520 m).
Weights: Empty equipped, 6,437 lb (2 920 kg); max. take-off, 11,243 lb (5 100 kg).
Accommodation: Pilot and co-pilot side-by-side on flight deck with full dual controls. Standard cabin arrangement provides six individual seats on each side of central aisle. Accommodation for four stretchers and two attendants.
Status: First of three prototypes flown October 26, 1968, with second and third following on October 19, 1969, and June 25, 1970, respectively. The first pre-series aircraft flew on August 15, 1972, and production tempo scheduled to attain four per month by July 1974 against an order for 80 aircraft for the *Fôrca Aérea Brasileira* and for government use.
Notes: Being manufactured by EMBRAER (Emprêsa Brasileira de Aeronáutica SA), the Bandeirante is intended to fulfil light transport, liaison, aeromedical and navigational tasks in the *Fôrca Aérea Brasileira*. The civil version of the Bandeirante has been ordered by Transbrasil and VASP.

EMBRAER EMB-110 BANDEIRANTE

Dimensions: Span, 50 ft 2¼ in (15,30 m); length, 46 ft 8¼ in (14,22 m); height, 15 ft 6 in (4,73 m); wing area, 312·13 sq ft (29,00 m²).

FAIRCHILD A-10A

Country of Origin: USA.

Type: Single-seat close-support aircraft.

Power Plant: Two 8,985 lb (4 075 kg) General Electric TF34-GE-100 turbofans.

Performance: Max. speed at 25,500 lb (11 567 kg), 461 mph (742 km/h) at sea level; max. design, 518 mph (833 km/h); mission radius (with 9,500 lb/4 309 kg useful payload and including 2 hrs loiter at 200 mph/322 km/h at 5,000 ft/1 525 m and 10 min combat at 345 mph/555 km/h at sea level), 300 mls (480 km) cruising at 357 mph (574 km/h) at 25,000 ft (7 620 m); ferry range, 2,648 mls (4 260 km).

Weights: Empty, 18,787 lb (8 522 kg); max. take-off, 45,202 lb (20 504 kg).

Armament: One 30-mm General Electric GAU-8/A cannon and up to 18,500 lb (8 392 kg) of ordnance on 11 external pylons. Typical possible loads include 24 Mk. 82 500-lb (227-kg) bombs, 16 M-117 750-lb (340-kg) bombs, four Mk. 84 2,000-lb (907-kg) bombs, 20 Rockeye 11 cluster bombs, or nine AGM-65 Maverick missiles.

Status: First of two prototypes flown May 10, 1972, followed by second on July 21, 1972. An initial batch of 10 is scheduled for delivery from December 1974, and October 1975 is the target for a decision on production beyond an initial batch of 40 aircraft.

Notes: Designed to meet the USAF's A-X close-support aircraft requirement, the A-10A participated in a fly-off contest with the Northrop A-9A (see 1972 edition) during the closing months of 1972 at which time eventual orders for up to 600 of the selected aircraft were anticipated. The A-10A was announced winning contender on January 18, 1973.

FAIRCHILD A-10A

Dimensions: Span, 55 ft 0 in (16,76 m); length, 52 ft 7 in (16,03 m); height, 14 ft 5½ in (4,41 m); wing area, 488 sq ft (45,13 m²).

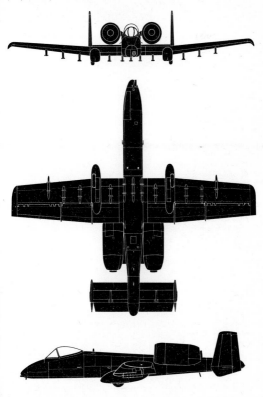

FOKKER F.27 FRIENDSHIP SRS. 500

Country of Origin: Netherlands.

Type: Short- to medium-range commercial transport.

Power Plant: Two 2,250 eshp Rolls-Royce Dart 532-7 turboprops.

Performance: Max. cruise, 322 mph (518 km/h) at 20,000 ft (6 095 m); normal cruise at 38,000 lb (17 237 kg), 298 mph (480 km/h) at 20,000 ft (6 095 m); range with max. payload, 667 mls (1 075 km), with max. fuel and 9,680-lb (4 390-kg) payload, 1,099 mls (1 805 km); initial climb at max. take-off weight, 1,200 ft/min (6,1 m/sec); service ceiling at 38,000 lb (17 237 kg), 29,500 ft (9 000 m).

Weights: Empty, 24,886 lb (11 288 kg); operational empty, 25,951 lb (11 771 kg); max. take-off, 45,000 lb (20 411 kg).

Accommodation: Basic flight crew of two or three and standard seating for 52 passengers. Alternative arrangements for up to 56 passengers.

Status: First Srs. 500 flown November 15, 1967. Production currently standardising on Srs. 500 and 600. Orders for the Friendship (including 205 licence-built in the USA by Fairchild) totalled 610 by beginning of 1974.

Notes: By comparison with basic Srs. 200 (see 1968 edition), the Srs. 500 has a 4 ft 11 in (1,5 m) fuselage stretch. The Srs. 400 "Combiplane" (see 1966 edition) and the equivalent military Srs. 400M are convertible cargo or combined cargo-passenger versions of the Srs. 200, and the current Srs. 600 (illustrated above) is similar to the Srs. 400 but lacks the reinforced and watertight cargo floor.

FOKKER F.27 FRIENDSHIP SRS. 500

Dimensions: Span, 95 ft $1\frac{3}{4}$ in (29,00 m); length, 82 ft $2\frac{1}{2}$ in (25,06 m); height, 28 ft $7\frac{1}{4}$ in (8,71 m); wing area, 753·47 sq ft (70 m²).

FOKKER F.28 FELLOWSHIP MK. 6000

Country of Origin: Netherlands.
Type: Short-range commercial transport.
Power Plant: Two 9,675 lb (4 390 kg) Rolls-Royce Spey Mk. 555-1H turbofans.
Performance: (At 70,000 lb/31 752 kg) 528 mph (849 km/h) at 21,000 ft (6 400 m); long-range cruise, 420 mph (676 km/h) at 30,000 ft (9 150 m); range with max. payload, 1,025 mls (1 650 km), with max. fuel (and 27 passengers), 1,197 mls (1 927 km).
Weights: Operating empty, 37,760 lb (17 127 kg); max. take-off, 70,000 lb (31 752 kg).
Accommodation: Flight crew of two with single-class accommodation for up to 79 passengers in five-abreast seating.
Status: The prototype Fellowship Mk. 6000 (the fuselage of the prototype Mk. 2000 and the modified wings of the second Mk. 1000 prototype) flew September 27, 1973, and production deliveries are scheduled for early 1975.
Notes: The Fellowship Mk. 6000 is a derivative of the stretched-fuselage Mk. 2000, offering improved field performance and payload/range capabilities. Wing span is increased by 4 ft 11½ in (1,50 m), three-section leading-edge slats are added to each wing, and an uprated, quieter version of the Spey engine is employed. Similar changes to the basic (shorter-fuselage) Fellowship Mk. 1000 will result in the Fellowship Mk. 5000. All four variants of the Fellowship are to be offered in parallel, and a large freight door is to be introduced for cargo or mixed passenger-cargo versions of the Mks 1000 and 5000.

FOKKER F.28 FELLOWSHIP MK. 6000

Dimensions: Span, 82 ft 3¾ in (25,09 m); length, 97 ft 1¼ in (29,61 m); height, 27 ft 9½ in (8,47 m); wing area, 850 sq ft (78,97 m²).

GAF NOMAD

Country of Origin: Australia.
Type: STOL utility transport.
Power Plant: Two 400 eshp Allison 250-B17 turboprops.
Performance: (Nomad 24 at 8,000 lb/3 629 kg) Max. cruise, 199 mph (320 km/h) at sea level, 202 mph (325 km/h) at 5,000 ft (1 524 m); long-range cruise, 161 mph (259 km/h) at 10,000 ft (3 048 m); max. range at 199 mph (320 km/h) at 10,000 ft (3 048 m) with 45 min reserves, 944 mls (1 518 km), with 1,600-lb (726-kg) payload, 725 mls (1 167 km) at max. cruise at sea level; initial climb, 1,500 ft/min (7,62 m/sec).
Weights: (Nomad 24) Basic empty, 4,330 lb (1 964 kg); max. take-off, 8,000 lb (3 629 kg).
Accommodation: Flight crew of either one or two, and up to 15 passengers in individual seats.
Status: First and second prototypes of Nomad 22 flown July 23, 1971, and December 5, 1971, respectively. Initial production batch of 20 Nomad 22s with first scheduled to fly early 1974. Approval given during 1973 for follow-on batch of 50.
Notes: Nomad 24 (general arrangement drawing) differs from Nomad 22 (second prototype of which is illustrated above) in having plugs in the fuselage fore and aft of the wing. Initial production batch confined to short-fuselage Nomad 22, and GAF (Government Aircraft Factories) to deliver 11 of first batch of 20 to Australian Army Aviation Corps. Four to be supplied to the Indonesian Navy.

GAF NOMAD

Dimensions: Span, 54 ft 0 in (16,46 m); length, 47 ft 0 in (14,30 m(; height, 18 ft 0 in (5,48 m); wing area, 320 sq ft (29,7 m²).

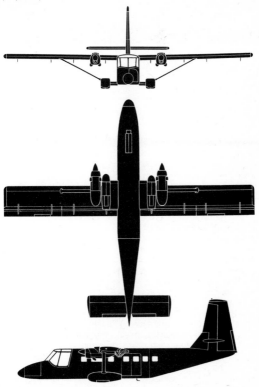

GATES LEARJET 35

Country of Origin: USA.

Type: Light business executive transport.

Power Plant: Two 3,500 lb (1 588 kg) Garrett AiResearch TFE 731-2 turbofans.

Performance: Max. speed, 548 mph (882 km/h); max. range, 3,028 mls (4 875 km); range with max. payload (1,914 lb/868 kg), 2,572 mls (4 140 km); initial climb, 5,150 ft/min (26 m/sec); service ceiling, 42,500 ft (12 950 m).

Weights: Operational empty, 9,142 lb (4 146 kg); max. take-off, 17,000 lb (7 711 kg).

Accommodation: Two pilots or pilot and passenger on flight deck and up to seven passengers in main cabin.

Status: Prototype Learjet 35 flown on August 22, 1973, with first customer deliveries scheduled to commence mid-1974. Production of all versions of Learjet running at seven per month at beginning of 1974.

Notes: The latest additions to the Learjet range, the Models 35 and 36, feature marginally longer fuselages and longer-span wings by comparison with the Model 25 which was previously the largest Learjet, and turbofans supplant the General Electric CJ610 turbojets employed by earlier models such as the Model 24D (see 1971 edition). The Models 35 and 36 are dimensionally similar, the latter accommodating up to six passengers and offering greater range (3,620 mls/ 5 826 km). Production of the Models 24D, 25B and 25C is continuing the 24D having a 43 ft 3 in (13,18 m) fuselage and the 25B and 25C being 4 ft 2 in (1,27 m) longer, the last-mentioned model possessing increased fuel capacity. The 400th Learjet (a Model 25B) was delivered in October 1973.

GATES LEARJET 35

Dimensions: Span, 39 ft 8 in (12,09 m); length, 48 ft 8 in (14,83 m); height, 12 ft 3 in (3,73 m); wing area, 253·3 sq ft (23,5 m²).

GENERAL DYNAMICS YF-16

Country of Origin: USA.

Type: Single-seat air superiority fighter.

Power Plant: One (approx.) 25,000 lb (11 400 kg) reheat Pratt & Whitney F100-PW-100 turbofan.

Performance: (Estimated) Max. speed, 1,320 mph (2 125 km/h) or Mach 2·0 at 40,000 ft (12 190 m); max. continuous cruise, 924–1,056 mph (1 485–1 700 km/h) or Mach 1·4–1·6 at 40,000 ft (12 190 m); service ceiling, 65,000 ft (19 810 m); combat radius, 575 mls (925 km) plus; ferry range, 2,300 mls (3 700 km).

Weights: Approx. empty, 12,000 lb (5 443 kg); normal take-off (including two AAMs, 17,500 lb (7 938 kg); max. take-off, 27,000 lb (12 247 kg).

Armament: One 20-mm M-61A rotary cannon with 500 rounds and two Raytheon AIM-9 Sidewinder AAMs.

Status: First of two prototypes for USAF evaluation was to commence flight test programme January 1974.

Notes: The YF-16 (Model 401) is one of two lightweight fighter designs selected for prototype construction by the USAF, the other being the Northrop YF-17 (see page 158). Lighter and smaller than the YF-17, the YF-16 is of blended wing-body concept in order to improve lift at high angles of attack. Manœuvring flaps provide automatic variable wing camber, and a fly-by-wire control system is employed.

GENERAL DYNAMICS YF-16

Dimensions: Span, 30 ft (9,14 m); length (excluding nose probe), 46 ft 11 in (14,30 m); height, 16 ft 3 in (4,95 m).

GRUMMAN A-6 INTRUDER

Country of Origin: USA.

Type: Two-seat shipboard low-level strike aircraft.

Power Plant: Two 9,300 lb (4 218 kg) Pratt & Whitney J52-P-8A turbojets.

Performance: Max. speed at 36,655 lb (16 626 kg) in clean condition, 685 mph (1 102 km/h) or Mach 0·9 at sea level, 625 mph (1 006 km/h) or Mach 0·94 at 36,000 ft (10 970 m); average cruise, 480 mph (772 km/h) at 32,750–43,800 ft (9 980–13 350 m); range with max. internal fuel and four Bullpup ASMs, 1,920 mls (3 090 km), with single store and four 250 Imp gal (1 136 l) external tanks, 3,040 mls (4 890 km).

Weights: Empty, 25,684 lb (11 650 kg); loaded (clean), 37,116 lb (16 836 kg); max. overload take-off, 60,280 lb (27 343 kg).

Armament: Max. external ordnance load of 15,000 lb (6 804 kg) distributed between five 3,600-lb (1 633-kg) stores stations.

Status: First of eight test and development aircraft flown April 19, 1960 and first delivery to US Navy (A-6A) on February 7, 1963.

Notes: Specification relates to basic A-6A (see 1970 edition), drawing depicts A-6B which differs in having equipment for AGM-78A Standard ARM (Anti-Radiation Missile). The A-6E has more advanced avionics and flew in prototype form on February 27, 1970, first deliveries to the US Navy following in 1971, with 72 funded by 1974 from planned total procurement of 192. Additional 192 A-6Es resulting from retrofit of A-6As.

GRUMMAN A-6 INTRUDER

Dimensions: Span, 53 ft 0 in (16,15 m); length, 54 ft 7 in (16,64 m); height, 15 ft 7 in (4,75 m); wing area, 529 sq ft (49,15 m²).

GRUMMAN EA-6B PROWLER

Country of Origin: USA.

Type: Four-seat shipboard electronic warfare aircraft.

Power Plant: Two 9,300 lb (4 218 kg) Pratt & Whitney J52-P-8A turbojets.

Performance: Max. speed, 599 mph (964 km/h) at sea level; average cruise, 466 mph (750 km/h); ferry range (with five 250 Imp gal/1 136 l external tanks), 2,475 mls (3 982 km); service ceiling, 38,000 ft (11 582 m).

Weights: Empty, 34,581 lb (15 686 kg); typical mission, 51,000 lb (23 133 kg); max. take-off, 58,500 lb (26 535 kg); max. overload, 63,177 lb (28 656 lb).

Accommodation: Forward cockpit housing pilot and electronic countermeasures operator side-by-side, and aft cockpit providing side-by-side seating for two additional countermeasures operators.

Status: Prototype EA-6B flown May 25, 1968, with first production deliveries to US Navy following in January 1971 with operational deployment commencing mid-1972. Total procurement of 65 (including one R & D and four pre-production) EA-6Bs by the US Navy anticipated.

Notes: Derived from the A-6 Intruder (see pages 90–91), the Prowler is intended to intercept, analyse, evaluate and jam hostile radar emissions. The primary mission is tactical stand-off jamming, and the Prowler carries 8,000 lb (3 629 kg) of avionics internally and a 950-lb (431-kg) avionics pod on the fuselage centreline and on four wing stations. The Prowler can also be used in the ECM escort or penetration roles. Current programme envisages 10 four-aircraft EA-6B squadrons.

GRUMMAN EA-6B PROWLER

Dimensions: Span, 53 ft 0 in (16,15 m); length, 59 ft 5 in (18,11 m); height, 16 ft 3 in (4,95 m); wing area, 529 sq ft (49,15 m²).

GRUMMAN E-2C HAWKEYE

Country of Origin: USA.

Type: Shipboard airborne early warning, surface surveillance and strike control aircraft.

Power Plant: Two 4,050 eshp Allison T56-A-8/8B turbo-props.

Performance: Max. speed, 356 mph (573 km/h) at sea level; normal cruise, 317 mph (510 km/h); on-station loiter speed, 161 mph (259 km/h); mission endurance, 7 hr, (at distance of 230 mls/370 km from base), 5 hr; ferry range, 1,722 mls (2 771 km); service ceiling, 28,100 ft (8 565 m).

Weights: Empty equipped, 37,616 lb (17 062 kg); max. take-off, 51,490 lb (23 355 kg).

Accommodation: Flight crew comprising pilot and co-pilot. Airborne Tactical Data System team of three.

Status: First of two E-2C prototypes flown on January 20, 1971, with production deliveries to the US Navy against initial procurement of 11 aircraft initiated early 1973. Follow-on procurement of eight from Fiscal 1973 funds and nine from Fiscal 1974 funds.

Notes: The E-2C is the current production version of the Hawkeye which first flew as an aerodynamic prototype on October 21, 1960. Fifty-nine examples of the E-2A (see 1968 edition) were delivered, all operational examples of this model subsequently being fitted with updated avionics as E-2Bs, the prototype of this variant having flown on February 20, 1969.

GRUMMAN E-2C HAWKEYE

Dimensions: Span, 80 ft 7 in (24,56 m); length, 57 ft 7 in (17,55 m); height, 18 ft 4 in (5,59 m); wing area, 800 sq ft (65,03 m²).

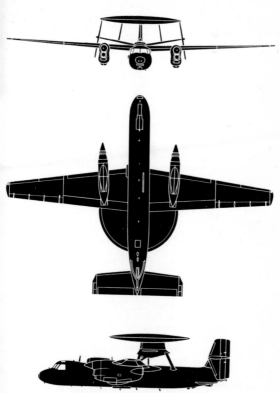

GRUMMAN F-14A TOMCAT

Country of Origin: USA.

Type: Two-seat shipboard multi-purpose fighter.

Power Plant: Two 20,900 lb (9 480 kg) reheat Pratt & Whitney TF30-P-412 turbofans.

Performance: Design max. speed (clean), 1,545 mph (2 486 km/h) at 40,000 ft (12 190 m) or Mach 2·34; max. speed (internal fuel and four AIM-7 missiles at 55,000 lb/24 948 kg), 910 mph (1 470 km/h) at sea level or Mach 1·2; tactical radius (internal fuel and four AIM-7 missiles plus allowance for 2 min combat at 10,000 ft/3 050 m), approx. 450 mls (725 km); time to 60,000 ft (18 290 m) at 55,000 lb (24 948 kg), 2·1 min.

Weights: Empty equipped, 40,070 lb (18 176 kg); normal take-off (internal fuel and four AIM-7 AAMs), 55,000 lb (24 948 kg); max. take-off (ground attack/interdiction), 68,567 lb (31 101 kg).

Armament: One 20-mm M-61A1 rotary cannon and (intercept mission) six AIM-7E/F Sparrow and four AIM-9G/H Sidewinder AAMs or six AIM-54A Phoenix and two AIM-9G/H Sidewinder AAMs. (Interdiction) Fourteen MK-82, eight MK-83 or four MK-84 bombs.

Status: First of 12 research and development aircraft flown December 21, 1970. Approx. 50 flown by beginning of 1974 when production was five–six per month. Total of 184 ordered by beginning of 1974 against anticipated procurement for US Navy of 313.

Notes: First of two F-14B prototypes powered by 28,096 lb (12 745 kg) reheat Pratt & Whitney F401-PW-400 turbofans flown on September 12, 1973. No production plans for this version existed at beginning of 1974.

GRUMMAN F-14A TOMCAT

Dimensions: Span (max.), 64 ft 1½ in (19,55 m), (min.), 37 ft 7 in (11,45 m), (overswept on deck), 33 ft 3½ in (10,15 m); length, 61 ft 11⅞ in (18,90 m); height, 16 ft 0 in (4,88 m); wing area, 565 sq ft (52,5 m²).

GRUMMAN AMERICAN AVIATION
AA-5 TRAVELER

Country of Origin: USA.

Type: Light cabin monoplane.

Power Plant: One 150 hp Avco Lycoming 0-320-E2G four-cylinder horizontally-opposed engine.

Performance: Max. speed, 150 mph (241 km/h) at sea level; cruise (75% power), 140 mph (225 km/h) at 9,000 ft (2 743 m); cruising range (at 75% power), 600 mls (966 km); optimum range, 650 mls (1 046 km); initial climb, 660 ft/min (3,35 m/sec); service ceiling, 12,650 ft (3 856 m).

Weights: Empty equipped, 1,304 lb (592 kg); max. take-off, 2,200 lb (998 kg).

Accommodation: Pilot and three passengers in paired separate seats beneath aft-sliding canopy.

Status: The prototype AA-5 Traveler was first flown on August 21, 1970, production deliveries following on FAA certification in December 1971. Combined production rate of AA-5 and AA-1B Trainer (which have some 60% commonality) was approx. 60 per month at beginning of 1974.

Notes: The AA-5 Traveler is essentially an enlarged version of the side-by-side two-seat AA-1B Trainer (see 1972 edition) powered by a 108 hp Avco Lycoming 0-235, and, apart from a more powerful engine, has a 7 ft (2,13 m) longer wing span and a 2·76 ft (84 cm) longer fuselage. Both the AA-1B Trainer and AA-5 Traveler are derivatives of the AA-1 Yankee low-cost two-seat sports monoplane.

GRUMMAN AMERICAN AVIATION AA-5 TRAVELER

Dimensions: Span, 31 ft 6 in (9,60 m); length, 22 ft 6¾ in (6,87 m); height, 8 ft 2½ in (2,50 m); wing area, 140 sq ft (13,01 m²).

HAWKER SIDDELEY 125 SERIES 600

Country of Origin: United Kingdom.
Type: Light business executive transport.
Power Plant: Two 3,750 lb (1 700 kg) Rolls-Royce Viper 601 turbojets.
Performance: Max. cruise, 518 mph (834 km/h) at 27,000 ft (8 230 m); long-range cruise, 503 mph (810 km/h) at 40,000 ft (12 192 m); range (max. fuel and 1,600-lb/725-kg payload plus 45 min reserves), 1,876 mls (3 020 km), (with 2,359-lb/1 070-kg payload), 1,785 mls (2 872 km).
Weights: Empty equipped, 12,148 lb (5 510 kg); max. take-off, 25,000 lb (11 340 kg).
Accommodation: Normal flight crew of two and basic arrangement for eight passengers with alternative arrangements available for up to 14 passengers.
Status: Two Series 600 development aircraft flown on January 21, 1971, and November 25, 1971. Production deliveries began early 1973.
Notes: The Series 600 is the current production version of the basic HS.125, this being essentially a higher-powered, stretched version of the Series 400 which it replaces. An additional 2-ft (0,62-m) section has been inserted in the fuselage ahead of the wing leading edge, this allowing two more seats to be offered in the cabin; a nose radome of improved profile has been adopted; the upper fuselage contours have been revised, and taller vertical tail surfaces have been adopted. Aircraft completed to US standards are being marketed in the USA by Beech as the BH.125-600A. Series 600 preceded by 101 Series 400 aircraft and 148 examples of earlier models plus two prototypes and 20 of a navigational training version (Dominie).

HAWKER SIDDELEY 125 SERIES 600

Dimensions: Span, 47 ft 0 in (14,32 m); length, 50 ft 5¾ in (15,37 m); height, 17 ft 3 in (5,26 m); wing area, 353 sq ft (32,8 m²).

HAWKER SIDDELEY 748 SERIES 2A

Country of Origin: United Kingdom.

Type: Short- to medium-range commercial transport.

Power Plant: Two 2,280 ehp Rolls-Royce Dart R.Da.7 Mk. 532-2L turboprops.

Performance: Max. speed at 40,000 lb (18 145 kg), 312 mph (502 km/h) at 16,000 ft (4 875 m); max. cruise, 287 mph (462 km/h) at 15,000 ft (4 570 m); econ. cruise, 267 mph (430 km/h) at 20,000 ft (6 095 m); range cruise, 259 mph (418 km/h) at 25,000 ft (7 620 m); range with max. fuel and reserves for 45 min hold and 230-mile (370-km) diversion, 1,862 mls (2 996 km), with max. payload and same reserves, 690 mls (1 110 km).

Weights: Basic operational, 25,361 lb (11 504 kg); max. take-off, 44,495 lb (20 182 kg).

Accommodation: Normal flight crew of two and standard cabin arrangement for 40 passengers on paired seats.

Status: First prototype flown June 24, 1960, and first production model (Series 1) on August 30, 1961. Series 1 superseded by Series 2 in 1962, this being in turn superseded by current Series 2A from mid-1967. Total of 335 (including 31 Andover C. Mk. 1 military transports for RAF) ordered by beginning of 1974.

Notes: Assembled under licence in India by HAL for Indian Airlines (24) and Indian Air Force (four Series 1, 41 Series 2 and 48 Series 2C) at rate of nine per year. The Series 2C flown on December 31, 1971, is similar to the Series 2A apart from the addition of a large rear freight door.

HAWKER SIDDELEY 748 SERIES 2A

Dimensions: Span, 98 ft 6 in (30,02 m); length, 67 ft 0 in (20,42 m); height, 24 ft 10 in (7,57 m); wing area, 810·75 sq ft (75,35 m²).

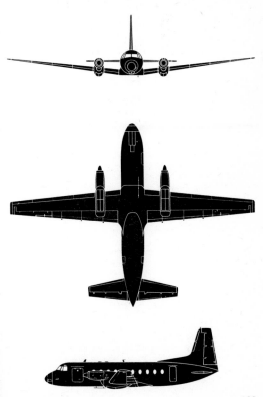

HAWKER SIDDELEY BUCCANEER
S. MK. 2B

Country of Origin: United Kingdom.

Type: Two-seat strike and reconnaissance aircraft.

Power Plant: Two 11,100 lb (5 035 kg) Rolls-Royce RB. 168-1A Spey Mk. 101 turbofans.

Performance: (Estimated) Max. speed, 645 mph (1 040 km/h) or Mach 0·85 at 250 ft (75 m), 620 mph (998 km/h) or Mach 0·92 at 30,000 ft (9 145 m); typical low-level cruise, 570 mph (917 km/h) or Mach 0·75 at 3,000 ft (915 m); tactical radius for hi-lo-lo-hi mission with standard fuel, 500–600 mls (805–965 km).

Weights: Max. take-off, 59,000 lb (26 762 kg).

Armament: Max. ordnance load of 16,000 lb (7 257 kg), including four 500-lb (227-kg), 540-lb (245-kg), or 1,000-lb (453,5-kg) bombs internally, and up to three 1,000-lb (453,5-kg) or six 500-lb (227-kg) bombs on each of four wing stations.

Status: First S. Mk. 2B for RAF flown January 8, 1970, with deliveries of 42 built to this standard continuing into 1974. Proportion of 84 S. Mk. 2s built for Royal Navy being modified for RAF use as S. Mk. 2As, and most of these ultimately to be converted to S. Mk. 2Bs.

Notes: The S. Mk. 2A embodies avionic, system and equipment modifications for RAF service. Wing and weapon-pylon changes to provide Martel missile capability characterise the S. Mk. 2B which introduces 425 Imp gal (1 932 l) fuel tank on rotating bomb door (seen on accompanying drawing) and undercarriage changes to accommodate new gross weight of 59,000 lb (26 762 kg). The Royal Navy versions are the S. Mk. 2C and S. Mk. 2D without and with Martel capability respectively.

HAWKER SIDDELEY BUCCANEER S. MK. 2B

Dimensions: Span, 44 ft 0 in (13,41 m); length, 63 ft 5 in (19,33 m); height, 16 ft 3 in (4,95 m); wing area, 514·7 sq ft (47,82 m²).

HAWKER SIDDELEY HARRIER G.R. MK. 3

Country of Origin: United Kingdom.

Type: Single-seat V/STOL strike and reconnaissance fighter.

Power Plant: One 21,500 lb (9 760 kg) Rolls-Royce Bristol Pegasus 103 vectored-thrust turbofan.

Performance: Max. speed, 720 mph (1 160 km/h) or Mach 0·95 at 1,000 ft (305 m), with typical external ordnance load, 640–660 mph (1 030–1 060 km) or Mach 0·85–0·87 at 1,000 ft (305 m); cruise, 560 mph (900 km/h) or Mach 0·8 at 20,000 ft (6 096 m); tactical radius for hi-lo-hi mission, 260 mls (418 km), with two 100 Imp gal (455 l) external tanks, 400 mls (644 km); ferry range with four 330 Imp gal (1 500 l) external tanks, 2,070 mls (3 330 km).

Weights: Empty, 12,400 lb (5 624 kg); max. take-off (VTO), 18,000 lb (8 165 kg); max. take-off (STO), 23,000+ lb (10 433+ kg); approx. max. take-off, 26,000 lb (11 793 kg).

Armament: Provision for two 30-mm Aden cannon with 130 rpg and up to 5,000 lb (2 268 kg) of ordnance on five external hardpoints.

Status: First of six pre-production aircraft flown August 31, 1966, with first of 77 G.R. Mk. 1s for RAF following December 28, 1967. Production of G.R. Mk. 1s and 13 T. Mk. 2s (see 1969 edition) for RAF completed. Production of 102 Mk. 50s (equivalent to G.R. Mk. 3) and eight two-seaters (equivalent to T. Mk. 4) for US Marine Corps continuing through 1974, first having been delivered January 26, 1971. Follow-on order for 15 G.R. Mk. 3s placed March 1973.

Notes: RAF Harrier G.R. Mk. 1s and T. Mk. 2s converted to G. R. Mk. 1As and T. Mk. 2As by installation of 20,000 lb (9 100 kg) Pegasus 102. These are to be progressively modified as G.R. Mk. 3s and T. Mk. 4s by installation of Pegasus 103 similar to that installed in Mk. 50 (AV-8A) for USMC. The G.R. Mk. 3s are to be fitted with nose-mounted laser rangefinder, new nose shape being illustrated above.

HAWKER SIDDELEY HARRIER G.R. MK. 3

Dimensions: Span, 25 ft 3 in (7,70 m); length, 45 ft 7$\frac{3}{4}$ in (13,91 m); height, 11 ft 3 in (3,43 m); wing area, 201·1 sq ft (18,68 m²).

HAWKER SIDDELEY HAWK T. MK. 1

Country of Origin: United Kingdom.

Type: Two-seat multi-purpose trainer and light tactical aircraft.

Power Plant: One 5,340 lb (2 422 kg) Rolls-Royce Turboméca RT.172-06-11 Adour 151 turbofan.

Performance: (Estimated) Max. speed (60% internal fuel), 600 mph (966 km/h) at sea level, 565 mph (910 km/h) at 32,810 ft (10 000 m); climb to 16,405 ft (5 000 m) with full internal fuel, 3·2 min.

Weights: Normal loaded (advanced trainer), 10,250 lb (4 650 kg), (weapon trainer), 12,000 lb (5 443 kg), (ground attack version), 15,610 lb (7 080 kg).

Armament: (Weapon trainer) One strong point on fuselage centreline and two wing strong points and (ground attack) two additional wing strong points. All points stressed for loads up to 1,000 lb (454 kg) each.

Status: Single pre-production example scheduled to fly during second quarter of 1974 with deliveries to RAF against current order for 175 aircraft commencing October 1976.

Notes: The Hawk T. Mk. 1 has been ordered by the RAF to provide basic jet training (taking over the portion of the present syllabus performed by the Jet Provost), advanced jet training (supplanting the Gnat) and weapons training (replacing the Hunter). Like the closely comparable Alpha Jet (see pages 68–69), the Hawk has been designed to have a ground attack (or light strike) capability and up to 5,000 lb (2 270 kg) of external ordnance will be carried by the ground attack variant which is intended primarily for export.

HAWKER SIDDELEY HAWK T. MK. 1

Dimensions: Span, 30 ft 10 in (9,40 m); length (including probe), 39 ft $2\frac{1}{2}$ in (11,96 m); height, 13 ft 5 in (4,10 m); wing area, 180 sq ft (16,7 m²).

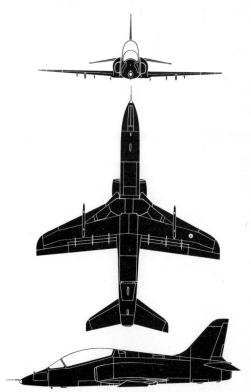

HAWKER SIDDELEY NIMROD M.R. MK. 1

Country of Origin: United Kingdom.
Type: Long-range maritime patrol aircraft.
Power Plant: Four 12,160 lb (5 515 kg) Rolls-Royce RB. 168-20 Spey Mk. 250 turbofans.
Performance: Max. speed, 575 mph (926 km/h); max. transit speed, 547 mph (880 km/h); econ. transit speed, 490 mph (787 km/h); typical ferry range, 5,180–5,755 mls (8 340–9 265 km); typical endurance, 12 hrs.
Weights: Max. take-off, 177,500 lb (80 510 kg); max. overload, 192,000 lb (87 090 kg).
Armament: Ventral weapons bay accommodating full range of ASW weapons (homing torpedoes, mines, depth charges, etc) plus two underwing pylons on each side for total of four Aérospatiale AS.12 ASMs (or AS.11 training rounds).
Accommodation: Normal operating crew of 12 with two pilots and flight engineer on flight deck and nine navigators and sensor operators in tactical compartment.
Status: First of two Nimrod prototypes employing modified Comet 4C airframes flown May 23, 1967. First of initial batch of 38 production Nimrod M.R. Mk. 1s flown on June 28, 1968. Completion of this batch in August 1972 followed by delivery of three Nimrod R. Mk. 1s for special electronics reconnaissance, and eight more M.R. Mk. 1s on order with deliveries commencing late 1974.
Notes: Entire fleet to undergo refit programme as Nimrod M.R. Mk. 2s with updated avionics and communications fit and service entry from 1977.

HAWKER SIDDELEY NIMROD M.R. MK. 1

Dimensions: Span, 114 ft 10 in (35,00 m); length, 126 ft 9 in (38,63 m); height, 29 ft 8½ in (9,01 m); wing area, 2,121 sq ft (197,05 m²).

HAWKER SIDDELEY TRIDENT 2E

Country of Origin: United Kingdom.
Type: Medium-haul commercial transport.
Power Plant: Three 11,930 lb (5 411 kg) Rolls-Royce RB.163-25 Mk. 512-5W/50 turbofans.
Performance: Max. cruise, 596 mph (959 km/h) at 30,000 ft (9 144 m); long-range cruise, 504 mph (891 km/h) at 35,000 ft (10 668 m); range with max. payload (29 600 lb/ 13 426 kg), 3,155 mls (5 077 km), with max. fuel at long-range cruise, 3,558 mls (5 726 km).
Weights: Operational empty, 73,200 lb (33 203 kg); max. take-off, 143,500 lb (65,090 kg).
Accommodation: Flight crew of three and alternative arrangements for 12 first-class and 79 tourist-class passengers or (BEA) 97 tourist-class passengers in six-abreast seating.
Status: Principal current production model of the Trident at the beginning of 1974 was the 2E which was being built against orders for 33 (plus two Super 3Bs) for the People's Republic of China. The first Trident 2E flew on July 27, 1967, 15 subsequently being delivered to British Airways (BEA) and two to Cyprus Airways.
Notes: The Trident 2E differs from the earlier Trident 1C and 1E (see 1966 edition) in having uprated engines, increased weights, Kücheman wingtips and increased span, fuel and weights. Twenty-four Trident 1Cs and 15 1Es were built. The Trident 3B (see 1973 edition) is a high-capacity short-haul development of the Trident 1E with a stretched fuselage and similar power plants and wing modifications to those of the 2E. Twenty-six Trident 3Bs were built for British Airways (BEA) with the last being delivered in April 1973.

HAWKER SIDDELEY TRIDENT 2E

Dimensions: Span, 98 ft 0 in (29,87 m); length, 114 ft 9 in (34,97 m); height, 27 ft 0 in (8,23 m); wing area, 1,462 sq ft (135,82 m²).

IAI-201 ARAVA

Country of Origin: Israel.

Type: Light Military transport and gunship.

Power Plant: Two 783 eshp Pratt & Whitney (UACL) PT6A-34 turboprops.

Performance: Max. speed (at 15,000 lb/6 803 kg), 203 mph (326 km/h) at 10,000 ft (3 050 m); max. cruise, 193 mph (310 km/h) at 10,000 ft (3 050 m); max. range (with 45 min reserves), 716 mls (1 153 km) at 9,840 ft (3 000 m); range with max. payload, 201 mls (323 km); initial climb, 1,338 ft/min (6,79 m/sec); ceiling, 25,000 ft (7 620 m).

Weights: Empty equipped, 8,300 lb (3 765 kg); max. take-off, 15,000 lb (6 803 kg).

Armament: One 0·5-in (12,7-mm) machine gun on each side of fuselage with 250 rpg, and provision for single aft-firing 0·5-in (12,7-mm) gun in flexible mount in the fuselage tail. Two hardpoints on fuselage are of 600-lb (272-kg) capacity and may carry such offensive stores as six-round 82-mm rocket pods.

Accommodation: Flight crew of one or two plus 23 fully-equipped troops or 16 paratroops and two despatchers. Eight casualty stretchers and three sitting casualties.

Status: Prototype IAI-201 began flight testing late 1971 with first production deliveries (to Mexican and Nicaraguan air forces) commencing mid-1973.

Notes: The IAI-201 is a military derivative of the IAI-101A (see 1972 edition), the former currently having production priority over the latter.

IAI-201 ARAVA

Dimensions: Span, 69 ft 6 in (20,88 m); length, 42 ft 7½ in (12,99 m); height, 17 ft 0¾ in (5,20 m); wing area, 470·2 sq ft (43,68 m²).

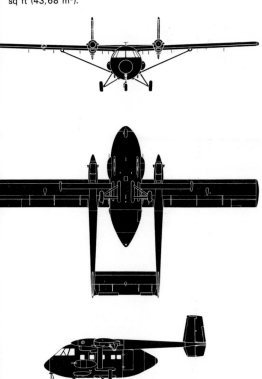

ILYUSHIN IL-38 (MAY)

Country of Origin: USSR.

Type: Long-range maritime patrol aircraft.

Power Plant: Four 4,250 ehp Ivchenko AI-20M turboprops.

Performance: (Estimated) Max. continuous cruise, 400 mph (645 km/h) at 15,000 ft (4 570 m); normal cruise, 370 mph (595 km/h) at 26,250 ft (8 000 m); patrol speed, 250 mph (400 km/h) at 2,000 ft (610 m); max. range, 4,500 mls (7 240 km); loiter endurance, 12 hrs at 2,000 ft (610 m).

Weights: (Estimated) Empty equipped, 80,000 lb (36 287 kg); max. take-off, 140,000 lb (63 500 kg).

Armament: Internal weapons bay for depth bombs, homing torpedoes, etc. Wing hardpoints for external ordnance loads.

Accommodation: Normal flight crew believed to consist of 12 members, of which half are housed by tactical compartment, operating sensors and co-ordinating data flow to surface vessels and other aircraft.

Status: The Il-38 reportedly flew in prototype form during 1967–68, entering service with the Soviet naval air arm early in 1970.

Notes: The Il-38 has been evolved from the Il-18 commercial transport in a similar fashion to the development of the Lockheed P-3 Orion from the Electra transport. Apart from some strengthening, the wings, tail assembly and undercarriage are similar to those of the Il-18. By comparison, the wing is positioned further forward on the fuselage for CG reasons.

ILYUSHIN IL-38 (MAY)

Dimensions: Span, 122 ft 9 in (37,40 m); length, 131 ft 0 in (39,92 m); height, 33 ft 4 in (10,17 m); wing area, 1,507 sq ft (140,0 m²).

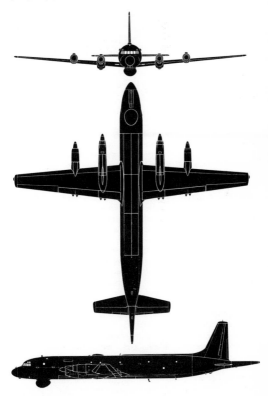

ILYUSHIN IL-76 (CANDID)

Country of Origin: USSR.

Type: Heavy commercial and military freighter.

Power Plant: Four 26,455 lb (12 000 kg) Soloviev D-30-KP turbofans.

Performance: Max. cruise, 528 mph (850 km/h) at 42,650 ft (13 000 m); range with max. payload (88,185 lb/40 000 kg), 3,107 mls (5 000 km).

Weights: Max. take-off, 346,122 lb (157 000 kg).

Accommodation: Normal flight crew of three—four on flight deck and in glazed nose, and pressurised hold for freight.

Status: First of four prototypes flown on March 25, 1971, with production deliveries to commence in 1974. Approximately 100 to be delivered to Aeroflot with initial service scheduled for late 1974.

Notes: Apparently evolved primarily to meet a military requirement, the Il-76 is generally similar in concept to the Lockheed C-141A StarLifter, but is slightly larger, more powerful and heavier. It employs a mechanised cargo-handling system, a high-flotation undercarriage, the main members of which comprise four individual units each of four parallel-mounted wheels, and extensive high-lift devices to achieve short-field performance. According to an official Soviet statement, the Il-76 is intended to operate from short unprepared strips in Siberia and other undeveloped areas of the Soviet Union during the period of the current five-year programme (1971–75). Clam-shell thrust reversers are fitted to all four power plants.

ILYUSHIN IL-76 (CANDID)

Dimensions: Span, 165 ft 8$\frac{1}{3}$ in (50,50 m); length, 152 ft 10$\frac{1}{4}$ in (46,59 m); height, 48 ft 5$\frac{1}{8}$ in (14,76 m).

KAWASAKI C-1A

Country of Origin: Japan.

Type: Medium-range military transport.

Power Plant: Two 14,500 lb (6 575 kg) Pratt & Whitney JT8D-9 turbofans.

Performance: Max. speed, 489 mph (787 km/h) at 25,000 ft (7 620 m); max. cruise, 426 mph (685 km/h) at 32,680 ft (10 670 m); range with max. fuel, 2,073 mls (3 335 km), with (normal) 17,637-lb (8 000-kg) payload, 806 mls (1 297 km); initial climb, 4,000 ft/min (20,3 m/sec); service ceiling, 39,370 ft (12 000 m).

Weights: Empty equipped, 53,131 lb (24 100 kg); max. take-off, 99,208 lb (45 000 kg).

Accommodation: Basic crew of five. Loads include 60 troops, 45 paratroops, or 36 casualty stretchers plus medical attendants. Cargo loads may include a 5,000-lb (2 268-kg) truck, a 105-mm howitzer, two 1,500-lb (680-kg) trucks, or three jeep-type vehicles.

Status: First of two flying prototypes flown on November 12, 1970, and second on January 16, 1971. First of two pre-production examples delivered 1973. Production deliveries scheduled to commence during the 1974 fiscal year in which three will be delivered to the Air Self-Defence Force. A further eight C-1As are expected to be delivered during the 1975 fiscal year against total procurement of 26 aircraft during the current (1972–75) five-year defence programme.

Notes: The C-1A is intended as a successor to the Curtiss C-46 transport, and a stretched version and an airborne early-warning derivative were being projected at the beginning of 1974.

KAWASAKI C-1A

Dimensions: Span, 100 ft $3\frac{3}{4}$ in (30,60 m); length, 95 ft $1\frac{3}{4}$ in (29,00 m); height, 32 ft $9\frac{3}{4}$ in (10,00 m); wing area, 1,297 sq ft (120,5 m²).

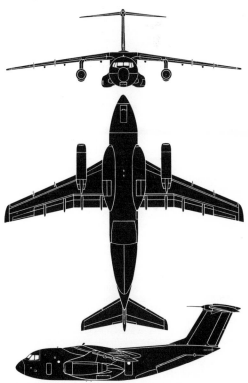

LET L 410 TURBOLET

Country of Origin: Czechoslovakia.
Type: Light utility transport and feederliner.
Power Plant: Two 715 eshp Pratt & Whitney PT6A-27 turboprops.
Performance: Max. cruise, 235 mph (380 km/h) at 9,840 ft (3 000 m); econ. cruise, 205 mph (330 km/h) at 9,840 ft (3 000 m); range with max. fuel and 45 min reserves, 705 mls (1 140 km), with max. payload and same reserves, 115 mls (185 km); initial climb rate, 1,595 ft/min (8,1 m/sec); service ceiling, 25,490 ft (7 770 m).
Weights: Empty equipped, 6,876 lb (3 100 kg); max. take-off, 11,905 lb (5 400 kg).
Accommodation: Basic flight crew of two. Configurations for 12, 15, 19 or 20 passengers in rows of three with two seats to starboard and one to port of aisle. Business executive layout available with accommodation for eight passengers.
Status: First of four prototypes flown April 16, 1969. Pre-production series of six aircraft built during 1971 of which two entered service with Slov-Air in September of that year. First production deliveries (to Slov-Air) commenced in 1972.
Notes: Principal production version of the Turbolet is to receive indigenous M-601-B turboprop of 740 eshp with which it was scheduled to commence flight testing during 1971. Latest modifications (see drawing) include redesigned wheel sponsons, a wider undercarriage track, revised engine nacelles and large ventral fin. Aeroflot was evaluating five aircraft during 1973 and is expected to order a substantial quantity during the course of 1974.

LET L 410 TURBOLET

Dimensions: Span, 57 ft 3 in (17,50 m); length, 44 ft 7½ in (13,61 m); height, 18 ft 4 in (5,65 m); wing area, 349·827 sq ft (32,5 m²).

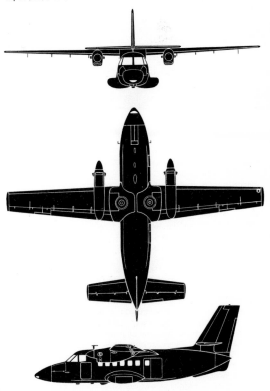

LOCKHEED JETSTAR II

Country of Origin: USA.

Type: Light business executive transport.

Power Plant: Four 3,700 lb (1 678 kg) Garrett AiResearch TFE 731-3 turbofans.

Performance: (Estimated) Max. cruise, 564 mph (908 km/h); long-range cruise, 504 mph (811 km/h); range, 3,185 mls (5 126 km) with 10 passengers; initial climb, 4,200 ft/min (21,3 m/sec); ceiling, 43,000 ft (13 106 m).

Weights: Operational empty, 23,578 lb (10 694 kg); max. take-off, 43,250 lb (19 618 kg).

Accommodation: Flight crew of two and maximum of 10 passengers in main cabin.

Status: Prototype JetStar II (converted from a JetStar I airframe by SAGA) was scheduled to commence its test programme early 1974. Production is expected to commence mid-1974 with first customer deliveries in April 1975.

Notes: The JetStar II is essentially a re-engined version of the Model 1329 JetStar (see 1964 edition), a total of 166 examples of which had been built when deliveries were completed in 1973. Early JetStars were powered by 2,400 lb (1 090 kg) Pratt & Whitney JT12A-6 turbojets, but examples delivered from 1967 were known as Dash 8 JetStars, having 3,300 lb (1 497 kg) JT12A-8 engines and embodying structural strengthening and various refinements. The JetStar II will offer a 40 per cent range increase.

LOCKHEED JETSTAR II

Dimensions: Span, 54 ft 5 in (16,60 m); length, 60 ft 5 in (18,42 m); height, 20 ft 5 in (6,23 m); wing area, 542·5 sq ft (50,40 m²).

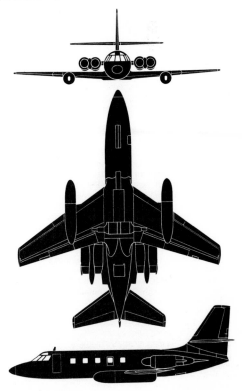

LOCKHEED L-1011-1 TRISTAR

Country of Origin: USA.
Type: Short- to medium-range commercial transport.
Power Plant: Three 42,000 lb (19 050 kg) Rolls-Royce RB.211-22B turbofans.
Performance: Max. cruise at max. take-off weight, 590 mph (950 km/h) at 35,000 ft (10 670 m); econ. cruise, 540 mph (870 km/h) at 35,000 ft (10 670 m); range with max. fuel and 40,000 lb (18 145 kg) payload, 4,467 mls (7 189 km); range with max. payload comprising 256 passengers and 5,000 lb (2 270 kg) cargo, 2,878 mls (4 629 km); initial climb, 2,800 ft/min (14,2 m/sec); service ceiling, 35,000 ft (10 670 m).
Weights: Empty, 218,999 lb (99 336 kg); operational empty, 234,275 lb (106 265 kg); max. take-off, 430,000 lb (195 045 kg).
Accommodation: Basic flight crew of three–four. Typical passenger configuration provides 256 seats in a ratio of 20% first class and 80% coach class. An all-economy configuration provides for 345 passengers, while up to 400 may be accommodated in a high-density configuration.
Status: First L-1011-1 flown November 16, 1970, with first deliveries (to Eastern) following in April 1972. By the beginning of 1974 orders and "second buy" options totalled 200 aircraft.
Notes: The Model 193 (L-1011) TriStar is the first aircraft to employ the RB.211 engine, and at the beginning of 1974 an extended-range version of the basic design with RB.211-24 engines was under study and was expected to go ahead during the course of the year.

LOCKHEED L-1011-1 TRISTAR

Dimensions: Span, 155 ft 4 in (47,34 m); length, 177 ft 8½ in (54,16 m); height, 55 ft 4 in (16,87 m); wing area, 3,755 sq ft (348,85 m²).

LOCKHEED C-130H HERCULES

Country of Origin: USA.
Type: Medium- to long-range military transport.
Power Plant: Four 4,050 eshp Allison T56-A-7A turbo-props.
Performance: Max. speed, 384 mph (618 km/h); max. cruise, 368 mph (592 km/h); econ. cruise, 340 mph (547 km/h); range (with max. payload and 5% plus 30 min reserves), 2,450 mls (3 943 km); max. range, 4,770 mls (7 675 km); initial climb, 1,900 ft/min (9,65 m/sec).
Weights: Empty equipped, 72,892 lb (33 063 kg); max. normal take-off, 155,000 lb (70 310 kg); max. overload, 175,000 lb (79 380 kg).
Accommodation: Flight crew of four and max. of 92 fully-equipped troops, 64 paratroops, or 74 casualty stretchers and two medical attendants. As a cargo carrier up to six pre-loaded freight pallets may be carried.
Status: The C-130H is the principal current production version of the Hercules which, in progressively developed forms, has been in continuous production since 1952, and at the beginning of 1974, when more than 1,300 Hercules had been ordered, production rate was three per month.
Notes: The C-130H, which was in process of delivery to the USAF, Zaïre, Morocco, Italy and Iran at the beginning of 1974, is basically a C-130E with more powerful engines, and the Hercules C Mk. 1 (C-130K), illustrated above, serving with the RAF differs in having some UK-supplied instruments, avionics and other items.

LOCKHEED C-130H HERCULES

Dimensions: Span, 132 ft 7 in (40,41 m); length, 97 ft 9 in (29,78 m); height, 38 ft 3 in (11,66 m); wing area, 1,745 sq ft (162,12 m²).

LOCKHEED P-3C ORION

Country of Origin: USA.

Type: Long-range maritime patrol aircraft.

Power Plant: Four 4,910 eshp Allison T56-A-14W turbo-props.

Performance: Max. speed at 105,000 lb (47 625 kg), 437 mph (703 km/h) at 15,000 ft (4 570 m); normal cruise, 397 mph (639 km/h) at 25,000 ft (7 620 ml); patrol speed, 230 mph (370 km/h) at 1,500 ft (457 m); loiter endurance (all engines) at 1,500 ft (457 ml), 12·3 hours, (two engines) 17 hrs; max. mission radius, 2,530 mls (4 075 km), with 3 hrs on station at 1,500 ft (457 m), 1,933 mls (3 110 km); initial climb, 2,880 ft/min (14,6 m/sec).

Weights: Empty, 62,000 lb (28 123 kg); normal max. take-off, 133,500 lb (60 558 kg); max. overload, 142,000 lb (64 410 kg).

Accommodation: Normal flight crew of 10 of which five housed in tactical compartment. Up to 50 combat troops and 4,000 lb (1 814 kg) of equipment for trooping role.

Armament: Weapons bay can house two Mk 101 depth bombs and four Mk 43, 44 or 46 torpedoes, or eight Mk 54 bombs. External ordnance load of up to 13,713 lb (6 220 kg).

Status: YP-3C prototype flown October 8, 1968, P-3C deliveries commencing to US Navy mid-1969 with 202 programmed of which 130 had been funded by 1974.

Notes: The P-3C differs from the P-3A (157 built) and -3B (144 built) primarily in having more advanced sensor equipment. Twelve P-3As have been modified as EP-3Es (illustrated above) for the electronic reconnaissance role, others have been adapted for the weather reconnaissance role as WP-3As, and a specially-equipped version, the RP-3D, is being used to map the earth's magnetic field.

LOCKHEED P-3C ORION

Dimensions: Span, 99 ft 8 in (30,37 m); length, 116 ft 10 in (35,61 m); height, 33 ft 8½ in (10,29 m); wing area, 1,300 sq ft (120,77 m²).

LOCKHEED F-104S STARFIGHTER

Country of Origin: USA.

Type: Single-seat interceptor and strike fighter.

Power Plant: One 11,870 lb (5 385 kg) dry and 17,900 lb (8 120 kg) reheat General Electric J79-GE-19 turbojet.

Performance: Max. speed, 910 mph (1 470 km/h) or Mach 1·2 at sea level, 1,450 mph (2 335 km/h) or Mach 2·2 at 36,000 ft (10 970 m); max. cruise, 610 mph (980 km/h) at 36,000 ft (10 970 m); tactical radius with two 162 Imp gal (736 l) and two 100 Imp gal (455 l) drop tanks, 740–775 mls (1 190–1 245 km); ferry range, 1,815 mls (2 920 km); initial climb, 50,000 plus ft/min (254 plus m/sec).

Weights: Empty equipped (interceptor), 15,006 lb (6 807 kg), (strike fighter), 15,761 lb (7 149 kg); loaded (clean), (strike fighter), 21,585 lb (9 791 kg); max. take-off, 31,000 lb (14 060 kg).

Armament: (Interceptor) One 20-mm M-61 rotary cannon, two AIM-7 Sparrow III and two AIM-9 Sidewinder AAMs.

Status: First of two Lockheed-built F-104S prototypes flown December 1966, and first Fiat-built production F-104S flown December 30, 1968. Production of 205 for Italian Air Force with 100th delivered in January 1973, and continuing at rate of two–three per month at beginning of 1974. Deliveries scheduled for completion in 1975.

Notes: Derivative of the F-104G (see 1966 edition) optimised for all-weather intercept role. Features uprated engine with redesigned afterburner. Nine external stores attachment points.

LOCKHEED F-104S STARFIGHTER

Dimensions: Span, 21 ft 11 in (6,68 m); length, 54 ft 9 in (16,69 m); height, 13 ft 6 in (4,11 m); wing area, 196·1 sq ft (18,22 m²).

LOCKHEED S-3A VIKING

Country of Origin: USA.

Type: Four-seat shipboard anti-submarine aircraft.

Power Plant: Two 9,280 lb (4 210 kg) General Electric TF34-GE-2 turbofans.

Performance: Max. speed, 506 mph (815 km/h) at sea level; max. cruise, 403 mph (649 km/h); typical loiter speed, 184 mph (257 km/h); max. ferry range, 3,500 mls (5 630 km) plus; initial climb, 3,937 ft/min (20 m/sec); service ceiling, 35,000 ft (10 670 m); sea level endurance, 8 hrs at 186 mph (300 km/h).

Weights: Empty equipped, 25,993 lb (11 790 kg); max. take-off, 41,963 lb (19 277 kg).

Accommodation: Pilot and co-pilot side by side on flight deck, with tactical co-ordinator and sensor operator in aft cabin. All four crew members provided with zero-zero ejection seats.

Armament: Various combinations of torpedoes, depth charges, bombs and ASMs in internal weapons bay and on underwing pylons.

Status: First of eight development and evaluation aircraft commenced its test programme on January 21, 1972, and remaining seven had flown by early 1973. Deliveries against follow-on orders for 93 scheduled for delivery at rate of four per month through 1976. Current US Navy planning calls for acquisition of 186 production aircraft.

Notes: Intended as a successor to the Grumman S-2 Tracker in US Navy service, Lockheed's shipboard turbofan-powered ASW aircraft was selected for development mid-1969 after competitive evaluation of a number of proposals, and was scheduled to enter fleet service early in 1974.

LOCKHEED S-3A VIKING

Dimensions: Span, 68 ft 8 in (20,93 m); length, 53 ft 4 in (16,26 m); height, 22 ft 9 in (6,93 m); wing area, 598 sq ft (55,56 m²).

McDONNELL DOUGLAS DC-9 SERIES 50

Country of Origin: USA.
Type: Short-to-medium-haul commercial transport.
Power Plant: Two 16,000 lb (7 257 kg) Pratt & Whitney JT8D-17 turbofans.
Performance: Max. cruise, 564 mph (907 km/h) at 27,000 ft (8 230 m); econ. cruise, 535 mph (861 km/h) at 33,000 ft (10 060 m); long-range cruise, 509 mph (819 km/h) at 35,000 ft (10 668 m); range with max. payload (33,000 lb/ 14 950 kg), 1,468 mls (2 362 km), with max. fuel (and 21,400-lb/9 700-kg payload), 2,787 mls (4 485 km).
Weights: Operational empty, 65,000 lb (29 484 kg); max. take-off, 120,000 lb (54 430 kg).
Accommodation: Flight crew of two/three and maximum high-density arrangement for 139 passengers in five-abreast seating.
Status: The first DC-9 Series 50 is scheduled to fly during the course of 1974 with first deliveries (against initial order for 10 from Swissair) following during the summer of 1975.
Notes: The latest of five basic DC-9 models, the Series 50 represents a further and presumably the ultimate ''stretch'' of the basic DC-9 airframe, the fuselage being 6·4 ft (1,95 m) longer than the previously largest DC-9, the Series 40. The DC-9 was first flown on February 25, 1965, and the 700th aircraft of this type was delivered in July 1973. Production versions include the initial Series 10, the Series 20 (see 1969 edition) retaining the short fuselage of the Series 10 with the longer-span wing of the Series 30 (see 1973 edition) and the Series 40 (see 1972 edition).

McDONNELL DOUGLAS DC-9 SERIES 50

Dimensions: Span, 93 ft 5 in (28,47 m); length, 132 ft 0 in (40,23 m); height, 27 ft 6 in (8,38 m); wing area, 1,000·7 sq ft (92,97 m²).

McDONNELL DOUGLAS DC-10 SERIES 30

Country of Origin: USA.

Type: Medium-range commercial transport.

Power Plant: Three 51,000 lb (23 134 kg) General Electric CF6-50C turbofans.

Performance: Max. cruise (at 520,000 lb/235 868 kg), 570 mph (917 km/h) at 31,000 ft (9 450 m); long-range cruise, 554 mph (891 km/h) at 31,000 ft (9 450 m); max. fuel range (with 230 mls/370 km reserves), 6,909 mls (11 118 km); max. payload range, 4,272 mls (6 875 km); max. climb rate, 2,320 ft/min (11,78 m/sec); service ceiling (at 540,000 lb/244 940 kg), 32,700 ft (9 965 m).

Weights: Basic operating, 263,087 lb (119 334 kg); max. take-off, 555,000 lb (251 745 kg).

Accommodation: Flight crew of three plus provision on flight deck for two supernumerary crew. Typical mixed-class accommodation for 225–270 passengers. Max. authorised passenger accommodation, 380 (plus crew of 11).

Status: First DC-10 (Series 10) flown August 29, 1970, with first Series 30 (46th DC-10 built) flying June 21, 1972, being preceded on February 28, 1972, by first Series 40. Orders and options totalled 235 by December 1973.

Notes: The DC-10 Series 30 and 40 have identical fuselages to the DC-10 Series 10 (see 1972 edition), but whereas the last-mentioned version is a domestic model, the Series 30 and 40 are intercontinental models, and differ in power plant, weight and wing details, and in the use of three main undercarriage units, the third (a twin-wheel unit) being mounted on the fuselage centreline. A convertible freighter version of the Series 30, the DC-10CF (illustrated above), was flown on February 28, 1973, being ordered by five airlines.

McDONNELL DOUGLAS DC-10 SERIES 30

Dimensions: Span, 165 ft 4 in (50,42 m); length, 181 ft 4¾ in (55,29 m); height, 58 ft 0 in (17,68 m); wing area, 3,921·4 sq ft (364,3 m²).

McDONNELL DOUGLAS F-15 EAGLE

Country of Origin: USA.

Type: Single-seat air-superiority fighter.

Power Plant: Two (approx.) 19,000 lb (8 618 kg) dry and 27,000 lb (12 247 kg) reheat Pratt & Whitney F100-PW-101 turbofans.

Performance: Max. sustained speed (approx.), 1,520 mph (2 446 km/h) or Mach 2·3 above 36,000 ft (10 975 m); max. short-period dash speed, 1,650 mph (2 655 km/h) or Mach 2·5; max. low-altitude speed (approx.), 915 mph (1 470 km/h) or Mach 1·2 at 1,000 ft (3 05 m).

Weights: Approx. max. loaded (air superiority mission), 40,000 lb (18 144 kg); max. take-off, 56,000 lb (25 400 kg).

Armament: One 20-mm M-61A-1 rotary cannon (eventually to be replaced by a 25-mm Philco-Ford GAU-7/A rotary cannon) and mix of four Raytheon AIM-7F Sparrow and four Raytheon AIM-9L Sidewinder AAMs.

Status: First of 20 development and test Eagles flown on July 27, 1972, with second and third following on September 26 and November 4, 1972, respectively. Eight of these 20 aircraft were being used during 1973–74 for service evaluation and 12 for the contractor's test programme. The Eagle is expected to enter the USAF inventory during 1975 and current planning calls for the purchase of 729 fighters of this type during Fiscal Years 1974–77.

Notes: Intended to provide the USAF with its principal air superiority capability during the period 1975–85, the Eagle is allegedly capable of climbing vertically at supersonic speed and of accelerating from subsonic cruise to speed of the order of Mach 1·5 within less than one minute.

McDONNELL DOUGLAS F-15 EAGLE

Dimensions: Span, 42 ft 9½ in (13,04 m); length, 63 ft 9½ in (19,44 m); height, 18 ft 7¼ in (5,67 m).

McDONNELL DOUGLAS F-4 PHANTOM

Country of Origin: USA.

Type: Two-seat interceptor and tactical strike fighter.

Power Plant: Two 11,870 lb (5 385 kg) dry and 17,900 lb (8 120 kg) reheat General Electric J79-GE-17 or (F-4F) MTU-built J79-MTU-17A turbojets.

Performance: (F-4E) Max. speed without external stores, 910 mph (1 464 km/h) or Mach 1·2 at 1,000 ft (305 m), 1,500 mph (2 414 km/h) or Mach 2·27 at 40,000 ft (12 190 m); tactical radius (with four Sparrow III and four Sidewinder AAMs), 140 mls (225 km), (plus one 500 Imp gal/2 273 l auxiliary tank), 196 mls (315 km), (hi-lo-hi mission profile with four 1,000-lb/453,6-kg bombs, four AAMs, and one 500 Imp gal/2 273 l and two 308 Imp gal/ 1 400 l tanks), 656 mls (1 056 km); max. ferry range, 2,300 mls (3 700 km) at 575 mph (925 km/h).

Weights: (F-4E) Empty equipped, 30,425 lb (13 801 kg); loaded (with four Sparrow IIIs), 51,810 lb (21 500 kg), (plus four Sidewinders and max. external fuel), 58,000 lb (26 308 kg); max. overload, 60,630 lb (27 502 kg).

Armament: One 20-mm M-61A1 rotary cannon and (intercept) four or six AIM-7E Sparrow IIIB plus four AIM-9D Sidewinder AAMs, or (attack) up to 16,000 lb (7 257 kg) of external stores.

Status: First F-4E flown June 1967, and production continuing at beginning of 1974. First F-4F (for Federal Germany) completed May 1973 with deliveries through 1974.

Notes: Current production models of the Phantom in addition to the F-4E (see 1973 edition) are the RF-4E (see 1972 edition), the F-4EJ for Japan and the F-4F for Federal Germany. The last-mentioned version (illustrated), optimised for the intercept role, was scheduled to enter service with the Luftwaffe from January 1, 1974, and features leading-edge slats and various weight-saving features.

142

McDONNELL DOUGLAS F-4 PHANTOM

Dimensions: Span, 38 ft 4¾ in (11,70 m); length, 62 ft 10½ in (19,20 m); height, 16 ft 3½ in (4,96 m); wing area, 530 sq ft (49,2 m²).

McDONNELL DOUGLAS A-4N SKYHAWK II

Country of Origin: USA.

Type: Single-seat light attack bomber.

Power Plant: One 11,200 lb (5 080 kg) Pratt & Whitney J52-P-408A turbojet.

Performance: Max. speed without external stores, 685 mph (1 102 km/h) or Mach 0·9 at sea level, 640 mph (1 030 km/h) at 25,000 ft (7 620 m), in high drag configuration, 625 mph (1 080 km/h) or Mach 0·82 at sea level, 605 mph (973 km/h) or Mach 0·84 at 30,000 ft (9 145 m); combat radius on internal fuel for hi-lo-lo-hi mission profile with 4,000 lb (1 814 kg) of external stores, 340 mls (547 km); initial climb, 15,850 ft/min (80,5 m/sec), at 23,000 lb (10 433 kg), 8,440 ft/min (42,7 m/sec).

Weights: Empty, 10,600 lb (4 808 kg); max. take-off, 24,500 lb (11 113 kg).

Armament: Two 30-mm DEFA cannon and external weapons loads up to 8,200 lb (3 720 kg) on wing and fuselage hardpoints.

Status: First A-4N flown June 12, 1972, with first production deliveries (to Israel) initiated November 1972.

Notes: The A-4N employs essentially the same power plant and airframe as the A-4M (see 1972 edition), both models being referred to as the Skyhawk II. The A-4N embodies some of the features originally developed for the Israeli A-4H (e.g., twin 30-mm cannon) but has a new nav/attack system (similar to A-7D and -7E) and a revised cockpit layout.

McDONNELL DOUGLAS A-4N SKYHAWK II

Dimensions: Span, 27 ft 6 in (8,38 m); length, 40 ft 3¼ in (12,27 m); height, 15 ft 0 in (4,57 m); wing area, 260 sq ft (24,16 m²).

MIKOYAN MIG-21MF (FISHBED-J)

Country of Origin: USSR.

Type: Single-seat multi-purpose fighter.

Power Plant: One 11,244 lb (5 100 kg) dry and 14,550 lb (6 600 kg) Tumansky R-11 turbojet.

Performance: Max. speed, 808 mph (1 300 km/h) or Mach 1·06 at 1,000 ft (305 m), 1,386 mph (2 230 km/h) or Mach 2·1 above 36,090 ft (11 000 m); range on internal fuel, 683 mls (1 100 km); ferry range with max. external fuel, 1,118 mls (1 800 km); service ceiling, 59,055 ft (18 000 m).

Weights: Normal take-off (with four K-13 AAMs), 18,078 lb (8 200 kg), (with two K-13s and two 110 Imp gal/500 l drop tanks), 19,731 lb (8950 kg); max. take-off (with two K-13s and three drop tanks), 20,723 lb (9 400 kg).

Armament: Two 23-mm cannon with 100 rpg in fuselage and up to four K-13 (Atoll) AAMs on wing pylons for intercept role. Four 550-lb (250-kg) bombs or four 220-mm or 325-mm ASMs.

Status: The MiG-21MF is a progressive development of the MiG-21PFM (*Fishbed-D*), and entered service with the Soviet Air Forces in the late 'sixties. Manufactured in parallel is a reconnaissance version (*Fishbed-H*), and licence manufacture is undertaken by HAL in India where 150 are being built at a rate of 30 per year from 1974.

Notes: The MiG-21MF is equipped with a boundary layer blowing system known as SPS. The *Fishbed-C* (MiG-21F) and *-E* are clear-weather interceptors, and the reconnaissance *Fishbed-H* features wingtip ECM fairings. The first Indian production equivalent of the MF is illustrated above.

MIKOYAN MIG-21MF (FISHBED-J)

Dimensions: Span, 23 ft 5$\frac{1}{2}$ in (7,15 m); length (including probe), 51 ft 8$\frac{1}{2}$ in (15,76 m), (without probe), 44 ft 2 in (13,46 m); wing area, 247·57 sq ft (23 m²).

MIKOYAN MIG-23 (FLOGGER)

Country of Origin: USSR.

Type: Single-seat interceptor fighter.

Power Plant: One (approx.) 28,000 lb (12 700 kg) reheat turbojet.

Performance: (Estimated) Max. speed, 865 mph (1 390 km/h) or Mach 1·2 at sea level, 1,520 mph (2 446 km/h) or Mach 2·3 at 39,370 ft (12 000 m), in high-drag configuration (e.g., two AAMs of advanced Anab type on fuselage stations and two AAMs on wing root stations), 1,120 mph (1 800 km/h) or Mach 1·7 at 39,370 ft (12 000 m); combat radius (with twin drop tanks on fuselage stations), 700 mls (1 126 km/h); service ceiling, 50,000 ft (15 250 m).

Weights: (Estimated) Normal take-off (with two AAMs), 30,000 lb (13 608 kg).

Armament: Two 23-mm or 30-mm cannon and up to four radar-guided AAMs on two fuselage and two wing root stations or mix of two infra-red homing and two radar guided AAMs.

Status: Prototypes believed flown 1967 with production commencing early 1971.

Notes: The MiG-23 is a variable-geometry fighter optimised for the air superiority role in limited operational service with the Soviet Air Forces from the beginning of 1973 and with avionics comparable with those of the F-4J phantom. The MiG-23B is a derivative of the basic design fulfilling the strike fighter role.

148

MIKOYAN MIG-23 (FLOGGER)

Dimensions: (Estimated) Span (minimum sweep), 48 ft 0 in (14,63 m), (maximum sweep), 24 ft 0 in (7,31 m); length (including probe), 60 ft 0 in (18,29 m).

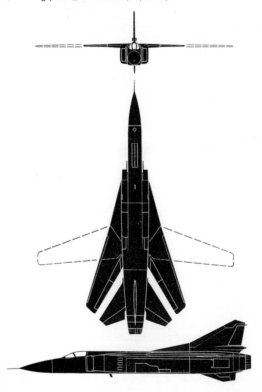

MIKOYAN MIG-25 (FOXBAT)

Country of Origin: USSR.

Type: Single-seat interceptor (Foxbat A) and reconnaissance fighter (Foxbat B).

Power Plant: Two (approx.) 24,250 lb (11 000 kg) reheat Tumansky turbojets.

Performance: (Estimated) Max. short-period dash speed, 2,100 mph (3 380 km/h) or Mach 3·2 at 39,370 ft (12 000 m); max. sustained speed, 1,780 mph (2 865 km/h) or Mach 2·7 at 39,370 ft (12 000 m), 975 mph (1 570 km/h) or Mach 1·3 at 4,920 ft (1 500 m); normal combat radius, 700 mls (1 125 km); time to 36,000 ft (10 970 m), 2·5 min.

Weights: (Estimated) Empty equipped, 34,000 lb (15 420 kg); normal loaded, 50,000–55,000 lb (22 680–24 950 kg); max. take-off, 64,200 lb (29 120 kg).

Armament: Four wing stations for radar homing AAMs for the intercept role. The MiG-25R (Foxbat B) has camera nose and no weapons pylons.

Status: Believed flown in prototype form 1963–64 with service deliveries following from 1970–71.

Notes: The MiG-25 multi-purpose fighter has established a number of FAI-recognised records since 1965 under the designation Ye-266. During 1973, the Ye-266 averaged, 1,619 mph (2 605 km/h) over a 100-km closed circuit, attained an altitude of 98,425 ft (30 000 m) in 4 min 3·9 sec, and established an absolute altitude record of 118,897 ft (36 240 m).

MIKOYAN MIG-25 (FOXBAT)

Dimensions: (Estimated) Span, 41 ft 0 in (12,5 m); length, 70 ft 0 in (21,33 m).

MITSUBISHI MU-2J

Country of Origin: Japan.

Type: Light business executive and utility transport.

Power Plant: Two 724 eshp Garrett AiResearch TPE 331-6-261M turboprops.

Performance: Max. cruise, 345 mph (555 km/h) at 15,000 ft (4 572 m); econ cruise, 304 mph (490 km/h) at 25,000 ft (7 620 m); max. range with 45 min reserves, 1,462 mls (2 350 km) at 22,965 ft (7 000 m); initial climb, 2,697 ft/min (13,7 m/sec); service ceiling, 30,775 ft (9 380 m).

Weights: Empty equipped, 6,800 lb (3 085 kg); max. take-off, 10,802 lb (4 900 kg).

Accommodation: Normal flight crew of two, and various cabin arrangements providing accommodation for from four to 12 passengers.

Status: Prototype MU-2J flown August 1970, deliveries of this model commencing late 1971. Parallel civil production model is the MU-2K, and final assembly of most civil aircraft is undertaken at San Angelo, Texas. Approximately 350 MU-2s of all versions had been built by 1974.

Notes: MU-2J is a more powerful version of the MU-2G (see 1971 edition) which, in turn, was a stretched variant of the MU-2F (see 1969 edition) with a re-positioned nosewheel and external main undercarriage fairings. The engines of the MU-2J are flat-rated at 665 hp up to 12,000 ft (3 660 m), and these are also employed by the current short-fuselage model, the MU-2K, which is otherwise similar to the MU-2F. Military models are the MU-2C (a non-pressurized version of the MU-2B) for liaison and reconnaissance/support roles with the Ground Self-Defence Force, and the MU-2E search and rescue version for the Air Self-Defence Force.

MITSUBISHI MU-2J

Dimensions: Span, 39 ft 2 in (11,95 m); length, 39 ft 5¾ in (12,03 m); height, 13 ft 8¼ in (4,17 m); wing area, 178 sq ft (16,55 m²).

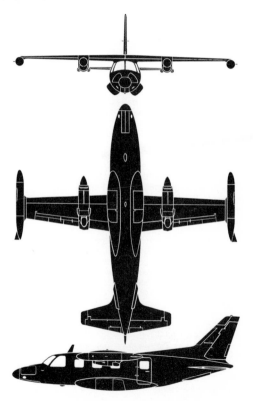

MITSUBISHI XT-2

Country of Origin: Japan.
Type: Tandem two-seat advanced trainer.
Power Plant: Two 3,810 lb (1 728 kg) dry and 7,070 lb (3 207 kg) reheat Rolls-Royce Turboméca RB.172-T.260 Adour turbofans.
Performance: (Estimated) Max. speed, 1,056 mph (1 700 km/h) or Mach 1·6 at 40,000 ft (12 190 m); max. ferry range, 1,600 mls (2 575 km); max. climb rate, 35,100 ft/min (178 m/sec); service ceiling, 50,000 ft (15 240 m).
Weights: Empty, 13,662 lb (6 197 kg); loaded (clean) 21,325 lb (9 673 kg); max. 25,274 lb (11 464 kg).
Armament: Provision for one 20-mm rotary cannon internally and various external ordnance loads on fuselage, underwing, and wingtip stations.
Status: First of four flying prototypes was flown on July 20, 1971, and all had been flown by the beginning of 1973. Current plans call for deliveries of 59 production T-2A trainers during the current five-year defence programme (1972–75).
Notes: Japan's first indigenous supersonic aircraft, the T-2A trainer is intended to enter the inventory of the Air Self-Defence Force in 1974. The basic design is also intended to fulfil operational roles, and the ASDF is to receive 68 examples of a close-support fighter version, the FS-T2Kai, these entering the inventory from 1976 onwards. A single-seater, the FS-T2Kai will carry a 20-mm rotary cannon and eight 500-lb (227-kg) bombs, two ASM-1 anti-shipping missiles or 12 500-lb (227-kg) bombs in overload condition. Max. take-off weight will be 30,865 lb (14 000 kg). The first ASDF training squadron to receive the T-2A is scheduled to be formed during 1975.

MITSUBISHI XT-2

Dimensions: Span, 25 ft 11 in (7,90 m); length, 58 ft $4\frac{3}{4}$ in (17,80 m); height, 14 ft $9\frac{1}{4}$ in (4,50 m); wing area, 228·2 sq ft (21,2 m²).

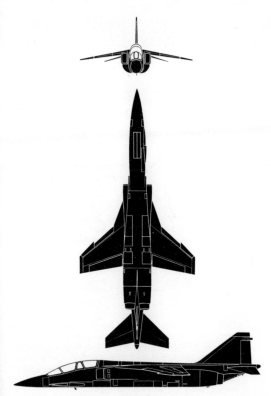

NORTHROP F-5E TIGER II

Country of Origin: USA.

Type: Single-seat air-superiority fighter.

Power Plant: Two 3,500 lb (1 588 kg) dry and 5,000 lb (2 268 kg) reheat General Electric J85-GE-21 turbojets.

Performance: Max. speed (at 13,220 lb/5 997 kg), 1056 mph (1 700 km/h) or Mach 1·6 at 36,090 ft (11 000 m), 760 mph (1 223 km/h) or Mach 1·0 at sea level, (with wingtip missiles), 990 mph (1 594 km/h) or Mach 1·5 at 36,090 ft (11 000 m); combat radius (internal fuel), 173 mls (278 km), (with 229 Imp gal/1 041 l drop tank), 426 mls (686 km); initial climb (at 13,220 lb/5 997 kg), 31,600 ft/min (160,53 m/sec); combat ceiling, 53,500 ft (16 305 m).

Weights: Take-off (wingtip launching rail configuration), 15,400 lb (6 985 kg); max. take-off, 24,083 lb (10 924 kg).

Armament: Two 20-mm M-39 cannon with 280 rpg and two wingtip-mounted AIM-9 Sidewinder AAMs. Up to 7,000 lb (3 175 kg) of ordnance (for attack role) on five external hardpoints.

Status: First F-5E flown August 11, 1972, and first deliveries February 1973. Production rate of 10 per month anticipated from early 1975.

Notes: A more powerful derivative of the F-5A (see 1970 edition) optimised for the air-superiority role, the F-5E won the USAF's International Fighter Aircraft (IFA) contest in November 1970, and the USAF has options on the production of up to 325 for supply under the Military Assistance Programme to South Korea, South Vietnam, Taiwan, Thailand and Jordan. Orders for the F-5E have also been placed by Brazil, Iran, Saudi Arabia and Malaysia. A tandem two-seat version, the F-5F, is under development.

NORTHROP F-5E TIGER II

Dimensions: Span, 26 ft 8½ in (8,14 m); length, 48 ft 2½ in (14,69 m); height, 13 ft 4 in (4,06 m); wing area, 186·2 sq ft (17,29 m²).

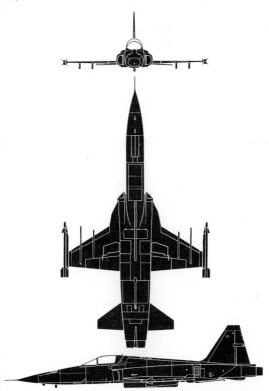

NORTHROP YF-17

Country of Origin: USA.

Type: Single-seat air superiority fighter.

Power Plant: Two 14,300 lb (6 486 kg) reheat General Electric YJ101-GE-100 turbojets.

Performance: (Estimated) Max. speed, 1,320 mph (2 125 km/h) or Mach 2·0 at 40,000 ft (12 190 m); max. continuous cruise, 1,056 mph (1 700 km/h) or Mach 1·6 at 40,000 ft (12 190 m); service ceiling, 65,000 ft (19 810 m).

Weights: Normal loaded (including two AAMs), 19,600 lb (8 890 kg); max. take-off, 21,000 lb (9 525 kg).

Armament: One 20-mm M-61A rotary cannon and two wingtip-mounted Raytheon AIM-9 Sidewinder AAMs.

Status: First of two prototypes for USAF evaluation scheduled to commence flight test programme April 1974.

Notes: The YF-17 is one of two lightweight fighter designs selected for prototype construction by the USAF with the object of determining through flight evaluation the possibilities of this warplane category, the other type ordered being the General Dynamics YF-16 (see page 88). The YF-17 (which has the company designation P-600) is essentially a partly defuelled derivative of the P-530 Cobra, a company-funded multi-purpose fighter that had reached an advanced project stage by the beginning of 1974. Externally the configurations of the YF-17 and P-530 are virtually identical, the latter embodying extra equipment, fuel and external warload. For the air superiority role the P-530 has a projected take-off weight of 23,000 lb (10 433 kg) with 5,800 lb (2 630 kg) of fuel, but seven external stores pylons can carry up to some 16,000 lb (7 260 kg) with which the P-530 will gross some 40,000 lb (18 145 kg). A projected shipboard strike fighter derivative is designated P-630.

NORTHROP YF-17

Dimensions: Span, 35 ft 0 in (10,67 m); length (excluding nose probe), 55 ft 6 in (16,92 m); height, 14 ft 6 in (4,42 m); wing area, 350 sq ft (32,51 m²).

NZAI CT-4 AIRTRAINER

Country of Origin: New Zealand.

Type: Side-by-side two-seat primary trainer.

Power Plant: One 210 hp Continental IO-360-D six-cylinder horizontally-opposed engine.

Performance: Max. speed, 183 mph (294 km/h) at sea level, 168 mph (270 km/h) at 10,000 ft (3 048 m); cruise (75% power), 158 mph (254 km/h) at sea level, 144 mph (232 km/h) at 10,000 ft (3 048 m), (55% power), 138 mph (222 km/h) at sea level; max. range (at 65% power), 824 mls (1 326 km) at 135 mph (217 km/h) at 5,000 ft (1 524 m), (with two 17·5 Imp gal/79,5 l wingtip tanks), 1,400 mls (2 253 km) at 5,000 ft (1 524 m); initial climb, 1,345 ft/min (6,8 m/sec).

Weights: Empty equipped, 1,520 lb (690 kg); design max. take-off, 2,350 lb (1 070 kg), (with tip tanks), 2,650 lb (1 202 kg).

Status: Prototype flown February 21, 1972, with first production (to Royal Thai Air Force) October 1973.

Notes: Manufactured by New Zealand Aerospace Industries (NZAI) formed in 1973 by the amalgamation of Aero Engine Services and Air Parts (NZ), the CT-4 has been ordered by the Royal Thai Air Force (24 examples), and by the Royal Australian Air Force (37 examples) with deliveries following on the completion of those to Thailand.

NZAI CT-4 AIRTRAINER

Dimensions: Span, 26 ft 0 in (7,92 m); length, 23 ft 2 in (7,06 m); height, 8 ft 6 in (2,59 m); wing area, 129 sq ft (12,00 m²).

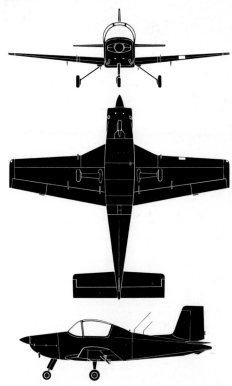

PANAVIA MRCA

Country of Origin: International consortium.

Type: Two-seat multi-purpose fighter.

Power Plant: Two 8,500 lb (3 855 kg) dry and 14,500 lb (6 577 kg) reheat Turbo-Union RB.199-34R turbofans.

Performance: Max. speed, 1,320+ mph (2 125+ km/h) or Mach 2·0+ above 36,000 ft (10 970 m), approx. 910 mph (1 465 km/h) at low altitude; combat endurance on internal fuel, approx. 70–80 min.

Weights: Empty equipped, 22,000–23,000 lb (9 980–10 430 kg); loaded, 38,000–40,000 lb (17 240–18 145 kg).

Armament: Two 27-mm Mauser cannon internally and various loads on three fuselage and four wing pylons.

Status: First of six prototypes was scheduled to fly March 1974, with remainder, together with three pre-production aircraft, to have joined the development programme by September 1975. Four of these development aeroplanes to be built in the UK, three in Federal Germany and two in Italy. Six further pre-production aircraft to be used in test programme and service deliveries to commence 1977–78 with current planning calling for 322 aircraft for the Federal German *Luftwaffe* and *Marineflieger*, some 385 for the RAF (of which approximately 165 will be optimised for the intercept role with the remainder being for interdiction strike), and about 100 for Italy's *Aeronautica Militare*.

Notes: The MRCA (multi-role combat aircraft) is being developed by Panavia Aircraft GmbH, a multi-national European industrial company formed by the British Aircraft Corporation, Messerschmitt-Bölkow-Blohm and Fiat.

PANAVIA MRCA

Dimensions: (Estimated) Span (max.), 42 ft 6 in (12,95 m), (min.), 27 ft 6 in (8,38 m); length, 52 ft 0 in (15,85 m); height, 19 ft 0 in (5,80 m).

PIPER CHEROKEE WARRIOR

Country of Origin: USA.

Type: Light cabin monoplane.

Power Plant: One 150 hp Avco Lycoming O-320 four-cylinder horizontally-opposed engine.

Performance: Max. speed, 135 mph (217 km/h); optimum cruise (75% power), 133 mph (213 km/h); optimum cruise range, 690 mls (1 140 km); initial climb, 649 ft/min (3,29 m/sec); service ceiling, 12,700 ft (3 930m).

Weights: Empty equipped, 1,301 lb (590 kg); max. take-off, 2,325 lb (1 065 kg).

Accommodation: Four persons in pairs with individual seats forward and bench-type seat aft.

Status: The Warrior, the latest in the PA-28 Cherokee series of light aeroplanes, was added to the current production range during the course of 1973 with deliveries commencing in November of that year.

Notes: Whereas all previous members of the Cherokee family of light cabin monoplanes have featured a constant-chord wing, the Warrior introduces a new tapered aerofoil section outboard of the flaps and a higher aspect ratio to reduce induced drag. The new wing is married to a fuselage essentially similar to that of the Cherokee Archer 180 (180 hp Avco Lycoming O-360-A3A) which it joins in the 1974 production range. Other members of the 1974 Cherokee range are the Pathfinder 235 (retaining the basic layout of the Archer 180 but having a 235 hp O-540-B4B5 engine), the Flite Liner two-seat trainer (150 hp O-320), the four-seat Arrow II and the six-seat Cherokee Six.

PIPER CHEROKEE WARRIOR

Dimensions: Span, 35 ft 0 in (10,65 m); length, 23 ft 9⅝ in (7,20 m); height 7 ft 3⅝ in (2,23 m); wing area, 170 sq ft (15,8 m²).

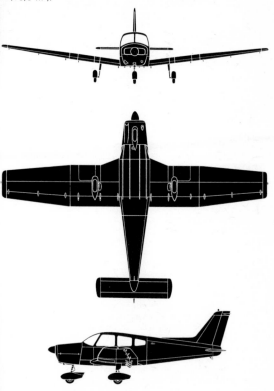

PIPER PA-34 SENECA

Country of Origin: USA.

Type: Light business executive transport.

Power Plant: Two 200 hp Lycoming IO-360-A1A four-cylinder horizontally-opposed engines.

Performance: Max. speed, 195 mph (314 km/h); optimum cruise at 75% power, 186 mph (299 km/h) at 6,000 ft (1 830 m), at 65% power, 183 mph (295 km/h), at 55% power, 178 mph (286 km/h); range at 75% power, 825 mls (1 340 km), at 65% power, 950 mls (1 525 km), at 55% power, 995 mls (1 600 km); initial climb, 1,360 ft/min (6,9 m/sec); service ceiling, 17,900 ft (5 450 m).

Weights: Empty equipped, 2,623 lb (1 189 kg); max. take-off, 4,200 lb (1 903 kg).

Accommodation: Standard accommodation for six persons in individual seats with alternative arrangement for seven persons with a three-across centre seat.

Status: Announced in September 1971 with deliveries commencing late same year, the Seneca has since been in continuous production, and the 1974 model (described and illustrated) introduces a fourth window in each side of the cabin and offers an aft utility door as standard.

Notes: The PA-34 Seneca is basically a twin-engined development of the single-engined PA-32 Cherokee Six, and is claimed by its manufacturers to be among the lowest-priced and largest-selling aircraft in its category. The 1974 model offers improved visibility and various new options such as an improved ventilation system, refined nosewheel steering and a "quietized" sound-proofing package.

PIPER PA-34 SENECA

Dimensions: Span, 38 ft 10¾ in (11,86 m); length, 28 ft 6 in (8,69 m); height, 9 ft 10¼ in (3,02 m); wing area, 206·5 sq ft (19,18 m²).

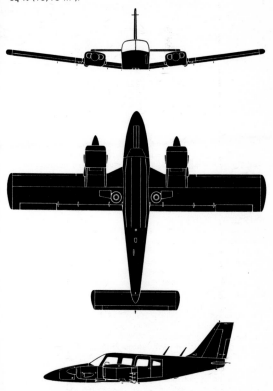

ROBIN HR 100-TIARA

Country of Origin: France.

Type: Light cabin monoplane.

Power Plant: One 320 hp Teledyne Continental 6-320 Tiara six-cylinder horizontally-opposed engine.

Performance: Max. speed, 208 mph (335 km/h) at sea level; cruise (75% power), 193 mph (310 km/h) at 9,840 ft (3 000 m); range (with four passengers), 948 mls (1 525 km), (with three passengers and no reserves), 1,398 mls (2 250 km); initial climb, 1,496 ft/min (7,6 m/sec); service ceiling, 19,685 ft (6 000 m).

Weights: Empty equipped, 1,765 lb (800 kg); max. take-off, 3,020 lb (1 370 kg).

Accommodation: Seating for four persons in pairs under canopy which slides forward to provide access to all seats.

Status: Prototype HR 100-Tiara flown for first time on November 18, 1972, with initial production deliveries following in the fourth quarter of 1973 when production of all versions of the HR 100 was five per month.

Notes: The HR 100-Tiara is a variant of the basic HR 100 Royale (see 1973 edition), from which it differs primarily in having a retractable undercarriage and the new Tiara engine. The HR 100, which first flew as a prototype on April 3, 1969, was the first all-metal aircraft to be produced by Avions Pierre Robin, and with a fixed undercarriage is currently available as the HR 100/180 (180 hp Avco Lycoming), HR 100/210 (210 hp Teledyne Continental) and HR 100/235, 250 and 260 (235, 250 and 260 hp Avco Lycoming). The retractable-undercarriage version is currently being manufactured with only the 320 hp 6-320.

ROBIN HR 100-TIARA

Dimensions: Span, 29 ft 9½ in (9,08 m); length, 24 ft 11 in (7,59 m); height, 7 ft 4½ in (2,25 m); wing area, 163·5 sq ft (15,2 m²).

ROBIN HR 200-100 CLUB

Country of Origin: France.
Type: Fully-aerobatic light cabin monoplane.
Power Plant: One 108 hp Avco Lycoming O-235-C2C four-cylinder horizontally-opposed engine.
Performance: Max. speed, 143 mph (230 km/h) at sea level; cruise (at 75% power), 133 mph (215 km/h) at optimum altitude, 124 mph (199 km/h) at sea level; range, 670 mls (1 080 km); initial climb, 669 ft/min (3,4 m/sec); service ceiling, 13,000 ft (3 962 m).
Weights: Empty equipped, 1,113 lb (505 kg); max. take-off, 1,680 lb (762 kg).
Accommodation: Pilot and passenger side-by-side on bench-type seat (with optional individual adjustable seats) beneath forward-sliding canopy.
Status: Prototype HR 200-100 flown July 30, 1971, with first production example following on April 16, 1973. The first examples of the HR 200-125 and HR 200-160 were flown in May 1973. Production of the HR 200 was scheduled to attain two per week at the beginning of 1974 when production plans called for the delivery of approximately 100 aircraft of this type during the course of the year.
Notes: An all-metal two-seater stressed for aerobatics, the HR 200 is an entirely original design possessing no more than a family resemblance to earlier products of Avions Pierre Robin and intended specifically for club and school use. The HR 200 Club is being offered with both the 108 hp engine (above) and the 125 hp Avco Lycoming (HR 200-125), and a third version known as the Acrobin (HR 200-160) has a 160 hp Avco Lycoming.

ROBIN HR 200-100 CLUB

Dimensions: Span, 27 ft 6½ in (8,40 m); length, 21 ft 11 in (6,68 m); height, 7 ft 1¾ in (2,18 m); wing area, 135·6 sq ft (12,6 m²).

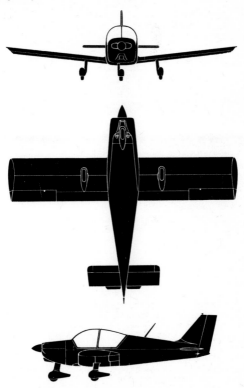

ROCKWELL B-1A

Country of Origin: USA.
Type: Strategic bomber.
Power Plant: Four (approx.) 30,000 lb (13 610 kg) General Electric F101-GE-100 turbofans.
Performance: (Estimated) Max. speed, 1,450 mph (2 335 km/h) at 40,000 ft (12 190 m) or Mach 2·2, 900 mph (1 450 km/h) at 1,500 ft (460 m) or Mach 1·2, 740 mph (1 190 km/h) at sea level or Mach 0·97; typical mission radius (at Mach 0·8) 3,600 mls (5 795 km); max. (un-refuelled) range, 6,100 mls (9 820 km).
Weights: Max. take-off, 389,800 lb (176 822 kg).
Armament: Twenty-four Boeing AGM-69A SRAM (Short Range Attack Missile) ASMs in three weapons bays or equivalent nuclear or conventional bombs plus additional SRAM ASMs on two external hard points.
Status: First of three prototypes scheduled to commence flight test programme July 1974 with third (avionics test) prototype flying in August 1975 and preceding second prototype scheduled to join test programme in January 1976.· Production decision expected to be taken July 1975 with initial deliveries to USAF Strategic Air Command in January 1978.
Notes: Comparable with the Soviet Backfire (see pages 204–205), the B-1A is intended as a successor to the B-52 Stratofortress in USAF Strategic Air Command service.

ROCKWELL B-1A

Dimensions: Span (max.), 136 ft 8½ in (41,66 m), (min.), 78 ft 2½ in (23,83 m); length, 143 ft 3½ in (43,68 m); height, 33 ft 7¼ in (10,24 m).

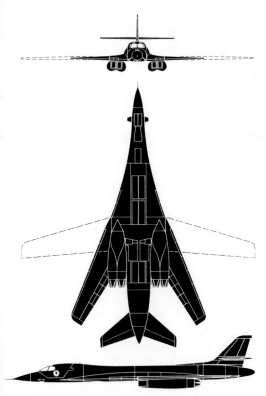

ROCKWELL XFV-12A

Country of Origin: USA.

Type: Single-seat shipboard V/STOL fighter.

Power Plant: One 14,070 lb (6 382 kg) Pratt & Witney F401-PW-400 turbofan (thrust boosted to 21,800 lb/9 888 kg for lift by augmentation system).

Performance: Estimated max. speed, 1,450 mph (2 330 km/h) at 40,000 ft (12 190 m) or Mach 2·2; operational radius (with max. fuel after 300 ft/91 m take-off roll), 575 plus mls (925 plus km).

Weights: Empty, 13,800 lb (6 260 kg); VTO take-off, 19,500 lb (8 845 kg); STO (300 ft/91 m) take-off, 24,250 lb (11 000 kg).

Armament: One 20-mm M-61 rotary cannon on fuselage centreline and four AIM-7 Sparrow AAMs or two AIM-7 and two AIM-9L Sidewinder AAMs.

Status: First of two prototypes scheduled to fly in the conventional mode in October 1974 with vertical trials commencing in January 1975.

Notes: The XFV-12A is an advanced technology prototype for a projected V/STOL fighter for use from the US Navy's proposed Sea Control Ships and utilising the TAW (Thrust-Augmented Wing) principle, this integrated lift/propulsion/control system facilitating conversion from hover to speeds in excess of Mach 2·0. The exhaust air from the turbofan is ducted to ejector flaps in the canard surfaces and wings, primary and ambient air being mixed and resulting in an augmentation ratio of 1·55. Hovering control is achieved by varying the diffuser geometry of each of the four lifting augmenters. To expedite the development programme, the XFV-12As utilise the A-4 Skyhawk forward fuselage and undercarriage and the F-4 Phantom wing box and air intakes.

ROCKWELL XFV-12A

Dimensions: Span, 28 ft 6 in (8,68 m); length, 43 ft 10 in (13,36 m); height, 9 ft 5 in (2,87 m).

ROCKWELL COMMANDER 112

Country of Origin: USA.

Type: Light cabin monoplane.

Power Plant: One 200 hp Avco Lycoming IO-360-C1D6 four-cylinder horizontally-opposed engine.

Performance: Max. speed, 175 mph (281 km/h) at sea level; cruise at 75% power at optimum altitude, 165 mph (265 km/h); range at 75% power (no reserves), 960 mls (1 545 km); optimum range, 1,130 mls (1 818 km); initial climb, 1,000 ft/min (5,08 m/sec); service ceiling, 17,000 ft (5 182 m).

Weights: Empty, 1,530 lb (694 kg); max. take-off, 2,550 lb (1 157 kg).

Accommodation: Pilot and three passengers seated in pairs with individual seats forward and bench seat aft.

Status: The first of five prototypes was flown on December 4, 1970, and customer deliveries commenced late 1972. A total of 270 was scheduled to be delivered by the end of 1973 when production exceeded 30 per month.

Notes: The development programme of the Commander 112 was somewhat protracted owing to modifications to the tail assembly necessitated by the loss of a prototype during high-speed diving trials. FAA certification being obtained during the course of 1972. The parallel Commander 111A (see 1972 edition) featured a fixed undercarriage and a 180 hp Lycoming O-360-A1G6 engine driving a constant-speed air-screw, but production is currently concentrated on the Commander 112 with production deliveries of the fixed-undercarriage model being scheduled to commence late 1974. A twin-engined version of the basic design is planned, and a six-seat version of the Commander 112 is projected.

ROCKWELL COMMANDER 112

Dimensions: Span, 32 ft 9 in (9,98 m); length, 24 ft 11 in (7,59 m); height, 8 ft 5 in (2,51 m); wing area, 152 sq ft (14,12 m²).

ROCKWELL SABRE 75A

Country of Origin: USA.
Type: Light business executive transport.
Power Plant: Two 4,315 lb (1 961 kg) General Electric CF700-2D-2 turbofans.
Performance: Max. cruise (at 21,370 lb/9 693 kg), 555 mph (893 km/h); long-range cruise, 488 mph (785 km/h); range (six passengers and 45 min reserves), 1,865 mls (3 000 km), (10 passengers and 45 min reserves), 1,695 mls (2 730 km); initial climb (at 23,000 lb/10 433 kg), 4,500 ft/min (22,86 m/sec).
Weights: Empty equipped, 13,200 lb (5 988 kg); max. take-off, 23,000 lb (10 433 kg).
Accommodation: Normal flight crew of two and various arrangements for six to 10 passengers.
Status: First prototype Sabre 75A flown initially on October 18, 1972, with second following on December 1, 1972.
Notes: The Sabre 75A is a variant of the Sabre 75 (see 1972 edition) which it replaces and from which it differs primarily in having turbofans in place of JT12A-8 turbojets, cascade-type thrust reversers, an increase in maximum fuel capacity, new high-energy disc brakes with an anti-skid system, and a new integral air-stair door. The Sabre 75A employs the same wings as those of the Sabre Commander 40A and the Sabreliner Series 60 (see 1968 edition) but has an entirely new fuselage of deeper section. Eleven Sabre 75As are on order for the US Federal Aviation Administration for navaid checking with deliveries commencing April 1974. The Sabre-liner series has been in continuous production for 15 years.

178

ROCKWELL SABRE 75A

Dimensions: Span, 44 ft 6 in (13,56 m); length, 47 ft 2 in (14,37 m); height, 17 ft 3 in (5,26 m); wing area, 342·05 sq ft (31,78 m²).

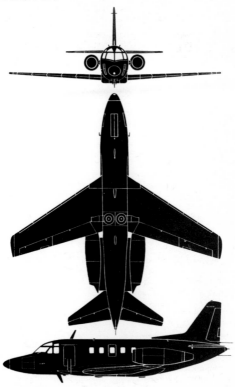

SAAB 37 VIGGEN

Country of Origin: Sweden.

Type: Single-seat multi-purpose fighter and two-seat operational trainer.

Power Plant: One 14,700 lb (6 667 kg) dry and 26,450 lb (12 000 kg) reheat Volvo Flygmotor RM 8 (Pratt & Whitney JT8D-22) turbofan.

Performance: (Estimated) Max. speed without external stores, 1,320 mph (2 125 km/h) or Mach 2·0 at 36,090 ft (11 000 m), 875 mph (1 410 km/h) or Mach 1·15 at 305 ft (100 m): tactical radius with typical external ordnance load for hi-lo-hi mission profile, 620 mls (1 000 km), for lo-lo-lo, 310 mls (500 km); time to 36,090 ft (11 000 m), 2 min.

Weights: Normal max. take-off, 35,275 lb (16 000 kg).

Armament: All ordnance carried on seven external stores stations, primary armament being RB 04E or RB 05A ASMs for the attack role, or RB 24 (Sidewinder) or RB 28 (Falcon) AAMs for the intercept role.

Status: First of six single-seat prototypes flown February 8, 1967, and two-seat prototype of training version flown July 2, 1970. Orders placed by beginning of 1972 for 150 single-seat (AJ 37) and 25 two-seat (SK 37) Viggens. First production Viggen flown February 23, 1971.

Notes: AJ 37 is primarily an attack aircraft with secondary intercept capability. Future versions include SF 37 tactical recce (illustrated) and SH 37 sea surveillance aircraft and JA 37 interceptor with an uprated RM 8B turbofan, new avionics and a built-in 30-mm Oerlikon KCA cannon.

SAAB 37 VIGGEN

Dimensions: Span, 34 ft 9¼ in (10,60 m); length, 50 ft 8¼ in (15,45 m), including probe, 53 ft 5¾ in (16,30 m); height, 18 ft 4½ in (5,60 m).

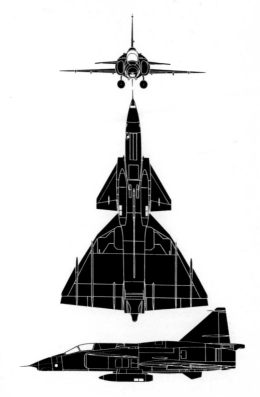

SAAB-MFI 15/17

Country of Origin: Sweden.

Type: Two-seat light utility, training and counter-insurgency aircraft.

Power Plant: One 200 hp Avco Lycoming IO-360-A1B6 four-cylinder horizontally-opposed engine.

Performance: Max. speed, 163 mph (262 km/h) at sea level; cruise at 75% power, 148 mph (238 km/h) at sea level; max. endurance at sea level (with 10% reserves), 4·75 hrs; max. climb rate, 1,555 ft/min (7,9 m/sec); service ceiling, 22,800 ft (6 950 m).

Weights: Empty equipped, 1,323 lb (600 kg); max. take-off, 2,094 lb.

Armament: (MFI 17) Six underwing hardpoints of which two inboard stressed for 220 lb (100 kg) and remainder for 110 lb (50 kg). Typical loads include four Abel pods each with seven 2·75-in (70-mm) HV rockets, six Bantam anti-tank missiles, 18 75-mm Bofors rockets or various gun pods.

Status: Prototype MFI 15 flown July 11, 1969, with first production deliveries (to Sierra Leone) begun April 1973.

Notes: The Saab-MFI 17 is essentially a version of the MFI 15 with provision for underwing stores and intended as a relatively inexpensive frontline support aircraft also suited for use for primary, instrument, aerobatic, navigation and weapons training. Space aft of the side-by-side seats may be occupied by a third seat facing to port, access and egress being provided by an upward-hinging door. The Saab-MFI 15 and 17 are being offered with both tricycle undercarriage and tailwheel arrangement.

SAAB-MFI 15/17

Dimensions: Span, 28 ft 6½ in (8,70 m); length, 22 ft 11½ in (7,00 m); height, 8 ft 6¼ in (2,60 m); wing area, 127 sq ft (11,8 m²).

SCOTTISH AVIATION BULLDOG 120

Country of Origin: United Kingdom.
Type: Side-by-side two-seat primary trainer.
Power Plant: One 200 hp Lycoming IO-360-A1B6 four-cylinder horizontally-opposed engine.
Performance: Max. speed, 150 mph (240 km/h) at sea level; max. cruise, 138 mph (222 km/h) at 4,000 ft (1 220 m); econ. cruise, 121 mph (194 km/h) at 4,000 ft (1 220 m); max. range, 628 mls (1 010 km) at 4,000 ft (1 220 m); initial climb, 1,100 ft/min (5,58 m/sec); service ceiling, 17,000 ft (5 180 m).
Weights: Empty, 1,420 lb (644 kg); max. take-off, 2,350 lb (1 065 kg).
Status: Beagle-built first prototype flown May 19, 1969. Scottish Aviation-built definitive prototype flying on February 14, 1971, with first production aircraft following July 1971.
Notes: Originally designed by the now-liquidated Beagle Aircraft, the Bulldog was taken over by Scottish Aviation, which has developed the aircraft for production. Production orders have been fulfilled for the Kenya (five Bulldog 103s), Royal Malaysian (15 Bulldog 102s), Ghanaian (six Bulldog 122s), Nigerian (20 Bulldog 123s) and Swedish (58 Bulldog 101s) air forces, and the Swedish Army (20), and an order for 132 for the RAF was in process of fulfilment at the beginning of 1974. The Bulldog 120 series is structurally strengthened to increase the fully aerobatic weight, and a wider range of instruments and avionics can be provided.

SCOTTISH AVIATION BULLDOG 120

Dimensions: Span, 33 ft 0 in (10,06 m); length, 23 ft 2½ in (7,07 m); height, 7 ft 5¾ in (2,28 m); wing area, 12·9·4 sq ft (12,02 m²).

SCOTTISH AVIATION JETSTREAM 201

Country of Origin: United Kingdom.
Type: Light business executive and utility transport.
Power Plant: Two 940 eshp Turboméca Astazou XVI turbo-props.
Performance: Max. cruise, 278 mph (448 km/h) at 12,000 ft (3 660 m), 254 mph (409 km/h) at 22,000 ft (6 705 m); range with max. fuel and 5% reserves plus 45 min hold, 1,382 mls (2 224 km); initial climb, 2,500 ft/min (12,7 m/sec); service ceiling, 26,000 ft (7 928 m).
Weights: Empty equipped (executive), 9,286 lb (4 212 kg); max. take-off, 12,550 lb (5 692 kg).
Accommodation: Normal flight crew of two and 12 passengers in executive layout with alternative 12–18 passenger commuter arrangements.
Status: Development initiated by Handley Page as the Jetstream 2, and flight testing resumed by Jetstream Aircraft Limited as the Jetstream Series 200 in December 1970. Production subsequently taken over by Scottish Aviation. Delivery of 26 pilot-training aircraft to the RAF commenced June 1973 as Jetstream T. Mk. 1.
Notes: The initial Handley Page-built version was the Jetstream 1 with Astazou XIV engines, 36 production examples of which were completed. Development of the Astazou XVI-powered Jetstream 2 was initiated by Handley Page with the re-engined first pre-production aircraft. All development is now being undertaken by Scottish Aviation and commercial deliveries will commence during 1974.

SCOTTISH AVIATION JETSTREAM 201

Dimensions: Span, 52 ft 0 in (15,85 m); length, 47 ft 1½ in (14,37 m); height, 17 ft 5½ in (5,32 m); wing area, 270 sq ft (25,08 m²).

SEPECAT JAGUAR G.R. MK. 1

Countries of Origin: France and United Kingdom.
Type: Single-seat tactical strike fighter.
Power Plant: Two 4,620 lb (2 100 kg) dry and 7,140 lb (3 240 kg) reheat Rolls-Royce Turboméca RT.172 Adour 102 turbofans.
Performance: (At typical weight) Max. speed, 820 mph (1 320 km/h) or Mach 1·1 at 1,000 ft (305 m), 1,057 mph (1 700 km/h) or Mach 1·6 at 32,810 ft (10 000 m); cruise with max. ordnance, 430 mph (690 km/h) or Mach 0·65 at 39,370 ft (12 000 m); range with external fuel for lo-lo-lo mission profile, 450 mls (724 km), for hi-lo-hi mission profile, 710 mls (1 142 km); ferry range, 2,270 mls (3 650 km).
Weights: Normal take-off, 23,000 lb (10 430 kg); max. take-off, 32,600 lb (14 790 kg).
Armament: Two 30-mm Aden cannon and up to 10,000 lb (4 536 kg) ordnance on five external hardpoints.
Status: First of eight prototypes flown September 8, 1968. First production Jaguar E for France flown November 2, 1971, with first Jaguar A following April 20, 1972. First production Jaguar S for UK flown October 11, 1972.
Notes: Both France and UK have a requirement for approximately 200 Jaguars, French versions being the single-seat A (*Appui Tactique*) and two-seat E (*École de Combat*), and British versions being the single-seat S (G.R. Mk. 1) and the two-seat B (T Mk. 2), current plans calling for the delivery of 165 single-seaters and 35 two-seaters to the RAF. The G.R. Mk. 1 differs from the Jaguar A in having a nose-mounted laser rangefinder and tail-mounted avionics pack.

SEPECAT JAGUAR G.R. MK. 1

Dimensions: Span, 28 ft 6 in (8,69 m); length, 50 ft 11 in (15,52 m); height, 16 ft 0½ in (4,89 m); wing area, 260·3 sq ft (24,18 m²).

SHIN MEIWA SS-2 (PS-1)

Country of Origin: Japan.

Type: Long-range maritime patrol flying boat.

Power Plant: Four 3,060 ehp Ishikawajima-built General Electric T64-IHI-10 turboprops.

Performance: Max. speed, 340 mph (547 km/h) at 5,000 ft (1 525 m); normal cruise, 265 mph (426 km/h) at 5,000 ft (1 525 m); normal range, 1,347 mls (2 168 km); ferry range, 2,948 mls (4 744 km); max. endurance, 15 hrs; initial climb, 2,264 ft/min (6,89 m/sec); service ceiling, 29,530 ft (9 000 m).

Weights: Empty equipped, 58,000 lb (26 300 kg); normal take-off, 79,366 lb (36 000 kg); max. take-off, 99,208 lb (45 000 kg).

Armament: Four 330-lb (150-kg) anti-submarine bombs on upper deck and additional weapons enclosed in two under-wing pods between engine nacelles (each containing two homing torpedoes) and a launcher beneath each wingtip (for three 5-in/12,7-cm rockets).

Accommodation: Two pilots and engineer on flight deck and seven additional crew members in tactical compartment on upper deck.

Status: First of two prototypes flown October 5, 1967, these being followed in 1972 by two pre-production examples. Initial batch of five production SS-2s delivered during 1973 and a further six are scheduled to be delivered before the end of 1975.

Notes: Three examples of an amphibious search and rescue version of the SS-2, the US-1 (alias RS-1), are currently on order for the Maritime Self-Defence Force with the first scheduled to fly autumn 1974.

SHIN MEIWA SS-2 (PS-1)

Dimensions: Span, 108 ft 8¾ in (33,14 m); length, 109 ft 11 in (33,50 m); height, 31 ft 10½ in (9,71 m); wing area, 1,462 sq ft (135,8 m²).

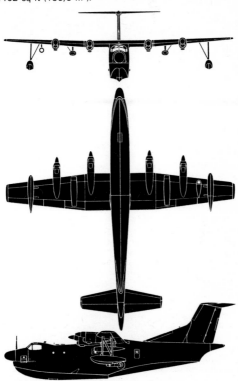

SHORT SKYVAN SERIES 3M

Country of Origin: United Kingdom.
Type: Light military utility transport.
Power Plant: Two 715 shp Garrett AiResearch TPE 331-201 turboprops.
Performance: Max. cruise, 201 mph (323 km/h) at 10,000 ft (3 050 m); econ. cruise, 173 mph (278 km/h) at 10,000 ft (3 050 m); range with max. fuel and 45 min reserves, 660 mls (1 062 km), with 5,000-lb (2 268-kg) payload and same reserves, 166 mls (267 km); initial climb, 1,520 ft/min (7,6 m/sec); service ceiling, 21,000 ft (6 400 m).
Weights: Basic operational, 7,400 lb (3 356 kg); max. take-off, 14,500 lb (6 577 kg).
Accommodation: Flight crew of one or two, and up to 22 fully-equipped troops, 16 paratroops and a despatcher, or 12 casualty stretchers and two medical attendants.
Status: Series 3M prototype flown early in 1970, and six delivered during course of year to Sultan of Oman's Air Force, this order being supplemented by orders for a further four. Five ordered for Argentine Navy, two for Nepalese Army, six for the Singapore Air Defence Command, six for the Ghana Air Force and one being ordered by the Ecuador Army. Interspersed on assembly line with civil Series 3, and combined production running at two per month at beginning of 1974 with total of 97 ordered.
Notes: The Series 3M (illustrated opposite with nose weather radar) is the military equivalent of the civil Series 3A.

SHORT SKYVAN SERIES 3M

Dimensions: Span, 64 ft 11 in (19,79 m); length, 40 ft 1 in (12,21 m), with radome, 41 ft 4 in (12,60 m); height, 15 ft 1 in (4,60 m); wing area, 373 sq ft (34,65 m²).

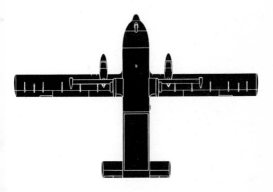

193

SHORT SD3-30

Country of Origin: United Kingdom.
Type: Third-level airliner.
Power Plant: Two 1,120 shp UACL Pratt & Whitney PT6A-45 turboprops.
Performance: (Estimated) High-speed cruise, 228 mph (367 km/h) at 17,000 lb (7 711 kg) at 10,000 ft (3 280 m), 224 mph (360 km/h) at 21,100 lb (9 570 kg) at 10,000 ft (3 280 m); long-range cruise, 184 mph (296 km/h); range (with 30 passengers and reserves for 45 min hold and 100 mls/160 km diversion), 253 mls (407 km) at high-speed cruise, 276 mls (444 km) at long-range cruise, (with 20 passengers), 737 mls (1 186 km) at high-speed cruise, 870 mls (1 400 km) at long-range cruise.
Weights: Empty equipped, 12,685 lb (5 753 kg); max. take-off, 21,100 lb (9 570 kg).
Accommodation: Flight crew of two and standard layout for 30 passengers in 10 rows three abreast. A total of 1,100 lb (500 kg) of baggage may be accommodated in aft and nose compartments.
Status: Prototype scheduled to fly August 7, 1974, with initial customer deliveries for September 1975 and planned production rate of four per month by end of 1976.
Notes: Owing much to the Skyvan, the SD3-30 is being optimised for commuter and regional air services. Wing design and construction are being undertaken by Fokker-VFW.

194

SHORT SD3-30

Dimensions: Span, 74 ft 9 in (22,78 m); length, 58 ft 0½ in (17,69 m); height, 15 ft 8 in (4,78 m); wing area, 453 sq ft (42,1 m²).

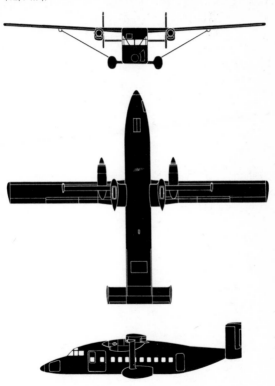

SIAI-MARCHETTI SF.260W WARRIOR

Country of Origin: Italy.

Type: Side-by-side two-seat light tactical and training aircraft.

Power Plant: One 260 hp Avco Lycoming O-540-E4A5 six-cylinder horizontally-opposed engine.

Performance: (Without external stores) Max. speed, 230 mph (370 km/h) at sea level; max. cruise, 214 mph (345 km/h) at 10,000 ft (3 050 m); econ. cruise, 203 mph (327 km/h) at 10,000 ft (3 050 m); max. range, 1,275 mls (2 050 km); initial climb, 1,770 ft/min (10 m/sec).

Weights: Empty equipped, 1,764 lb (800 kg); max. take-off, 2,879–2998 lb (1 306–1 360 kg).

Armament: Stores pylons for maximum of 661 lb (300 kg) of ordnance. Typical ordnance loads comprise two Matra gun pods each containing two 7,62-mm MAC AAF1 machine guns, two Alkan 20AP cartridge throwers, two Simpres AL18-50 pods each containing 18 2-in (5,0-cm) rockets or AL9-70 pods each containing nine 2·75-in (6,98-cm) rockets, or two 110-lb (50-kg) or 264·5-lb (120-kg) bombs.

Status: The prototype SF.260W was flown for the first time in May 1972. Production of SF.260 and SF.260W continuing at beginning of 1974.

Notes: The Warrior is an armed version of the SF.260MX trainer, the generic designation of the export military version of the SF.260 cabin monoplane of which deliveries commenced in 1970. The SF.260MX has been supplied to Belgium (36), Zaïre (12), Zambia (10), Singapore (18), Philippines (48 including 16 SF.260Ws) and Thailand (12 plus an option on a further 12).

SIAI-MARCHETTI SF.260W WARRIOR

Dimensions: Span, 26 ft 11¾ in (8,25 m); length, 23 ft 0 in (7,02 m); height, 8 ft 6 in (2,60 m); wing area, 108·5 sq ft (10,1 m²).

SIAI-MARCHETTI SM.1019A

Country of Origin: Italy.

Type: Battlefield surveillance and forward air control aircraft.

Power Plant: One 317 shp Allison 250-B15G turboprop.

Performance: Max. speed (at 2,293 lb/1 040 kg), 182 mph (293 km/h) at sea level; max. cruise, 173 mph (278 km/h) at 6,000 ft (1 830 m); econ. cruise, 135 mph (217 km/h) at 10,000 ft (3 050 m); range with max. fuel and 10 min reserves, 765 mls (1 230 km), with 500-lb (227-kg) external stores on wing stations and same reserves, 320 mls (515 km); initial climb, 1,625 ft (8,25 m/sec).

Weights: Empty equipped, 1,499 lb (680 kg); max. take-off, 2,513 lb (1 140 kg).

Armament: Two stores stations under wings capable of carrying minigun pods, rockets, etc., up to a maximum external load of 500 lb (227 kg).

Status: First of two prototypes flown May 24, 1969 and second on July 14, 1970. A production line for 100 aircraft was laid down late 1973 with first production aircraft scheduled to fly mid-1974.

Notes: The SM.1019 is based upon the Cessna O-1 Bird Dog but possesses an extensively modified airframe to meet latest operational requirements, redesigned tail surfaces, and a turboprop in place of the O-1's piston engine. The second prototype, the SM.1019A, has a second door for the observer and duplicated instrument panel. The SM.1019 competed with the AM.3C (see pages 6–7) for a production order for the Italian Army, and was selected as the winning contender.

SIAI-MARCHETTI SM.1019A

Dimensions: Span, 36 ft 0 in (10,97 m); length, 27 ft 10⅔ in (8,52 m); height, 7 ft 9¼ in (2,38 m); wing area, 173·94 sq ft (16,16 m²).

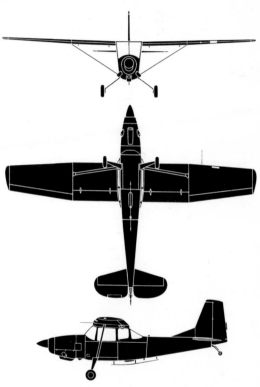

SMITH SUPERSTAR 700

Country of Origin: USA.

Type: Light business executive transport.

Power Plant: Two 300 hp Lycoming IO-540-M six-cylinder horizontally-opposed engines.

Performance: Max. speed, 275 mph (442 km/h) at sea level; cruise (70% power), 255 mph (410 km/h) at 10,000 ft (3 050 m), (55% power), 178 mph (286 km/h) at 10,000 ft (3 050 m); range, 1,100 mls (1 770 km) at 255 mph (410 km/h), 1,600 mls (2 575 km) at 178 mph (286 km/h); initial climb, 2,480 ft/min (12,6 m/sec).

Weights: Empty, 3,900 lb (1 770 kg); max. take-off, 6,300 lb (2 857 kg).

Accommodation: Pilot and five passenger seats in pairs.

Status: Prototype Superstar 700 flown November 22, 1972, and first deliveries scheduled for late 1974.

Notes: The Superstar 700 complements the current (and externally similar) Aerostar range being manufactured by Ted R. Smith and Associates, these comprising the Aerostar 600 with normally aspirated Lycoming IO-540s, the Aerostar 601 with turbo-supercharged IO-540s and the pressurised Aerostar 601P. The Superstar 700 is more powerful and marginally larger and heavier than the Aerostar and conforms to the same philosophy of using a minimum of detail parts and deriving strength from heavy skin gauges throughout the structure, coupled with maximum interchangeability between various components. The Superstar 700P will have turbo-supercharged engines and cabin pressurisation.

SMITH SUPERSTAR 700

Dimensions: Span, 36 ft 8 in (11,18 m); length, 35 ft 4 in (10,77 m); wing area, 193·54 sq ft (17,96 m²).

SUKHOI SU-15 (FLAGON-A)

Country of Origin: USSR.

Type: Single-seat all-weather interceptor fighter.

Power Plant: Two (approx.) 25,000 lb (11 340 kg) reheat Lyulka AL-9 turbojets.

Performance: (Estimated) Max. speed without external stores, 1,650 mph (2 655 km/h) or Mach 2·5 at 39,370 ft (12 000 m), 910 mph (1 465 km/h) or Mach 1·2 at 1,000 ft (305 m), with AAMs on wing stations and twin drop tanks on fuselage stations, 1,120 mph (1 800 km/h) or Mach 1·7 at 39,370 ft (12 000 m); range at subsonic cruise with max. external fuel, 1,500 mls (2 415 km).

Weights: (Estimated) Normal take-off, 35,000–40,000 lb (15 875–18 145 kg).

Armament: Basic armament for intercept mission reportedly comprises two AAMs of Anab type on wing stations, but various ordnance loads may be carried for the attack role, these being distributed between two fuselage and two wing stations.

Status: The Su-15 is believed to have flown in prototype form during 1964–65 with production deliveries commencing 1969, and some 400 were alleged by US official sources to be in service with the Soviet Air Forces by mid-1971 when production was believed to be some 15 aircraft monthly.

Notes: Apparently optimised for the intercept role as a successor to the Su-9 (see 1973 edition), the Su-15 is in large-scale service with the Soviet Air Forces. A STOL version with three direct lift engines in the centre fuselage, the Flagon-B, is of uncertain status. The Flagon was originally thought to have been designated Su-11, this designation now being known to apply to a developed version of the Su-9.

SUKHOI SU-15 (FLAGON-A)

Dimensions: (Estimated) Span, 31 ft 3 in (9,50 m); length, 70 ft 6 in (21,50 m); height, 16 ft 6 in (5,00 m).

203

TUPOLEV (BACKFIRE)

Country of Origin: USSR.
Type: Strategic bomber.
Power Plant: Two (approx.) 40,000 lb (18 144 kg) reheat Kuznetsov turbofans.
Performance: (Estimated) Max. speed, 1,450–1,650 mph (2 330–2 655 km/h) at 40,000 ft (12 190 m) or Mach 2·2–2·5; range (at subsonic speed), 4,500 plus mls (7 240 plus km).
Weights: Loaded (approx.), 275,000 lb (124 740 kg).
Armament: Primary attack armament comprises one ASM-6 stand-off missile with range of approx. 460 mls (740 km).
Status: First reported 1969 and believed to be in early service phase-in stage at beginning of 1974.
Notes: Believed to match the anticipated performance of the Rockwell B-1 (see pages 172–173) in key areas, the Backfire is reportedly a design of the Tupolev bureau. Equivalent of two USAF squadrons allegedly in service by beginning of 1974.

TUPOLEV (BACKFIRE)

Dimensions: No details available for publication.

TUPOLEV (MOSS)

Country of Origin: USSR.

Type: Airborne warning and control system aircraft.

Power Plant: Four 14,795 ehp Kuznetsov NK-12MV turbo-props.

Performance: (Estimated) Max. continuous cruise, 460 mph (740 km/h) at 25,000 ft (7 620 m); max. unrefuelled range, 4,000+ mls (6 440+ km); service ceiling, 39,000 ft (11 890 m).

Weights: (Estimated) Normal max. take-off, 360,000 lb (163 290 kg).

Accommodation: Operational crew is likely to comprise 15–20 personnel.

Status: The AWACS aircraft assigned the reporting name *Moss* by the Air Standards Co-ordinating Committee became known to Western intelligence agencies in the mid 'sixties, and first appeared in service in 1970.

Notes: Essentially an adaptation of the Tu-114 commercial transport, and apparently retaining the wings, tail surfaces, power plant and undercarriage of the earlier aircraft, the Tupolev AWACS type is primarily intended to locate low-flying intruders and to vector interceptors towards them. The dominating feature of the aircraft is its pylon-mounted saucer-shaped early-warning scanner housing of approximately 37·5 ft (12,00 m) diameter.

TUPOLEV (MOSS)

Dimensions: Span, 168 ft 0 in (51,20 m); approx. length, 188 ft 0 in (57,30 m); height, 51 ft 0 in (15,50 m); wing area, 3,349 sq ft (311,1 m²).

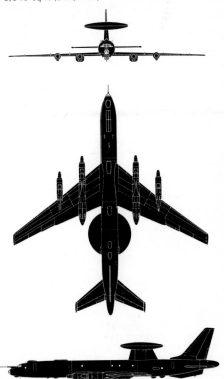

TUPOLEV TU-22 (BLINDER)

Country of Origin: USSR.

Type: Long-range medium bomber and strike-reconnaissance aircraft.

Power Plant: Two (approx.) 27,000 lb (12 250 kg) reheat turbojets.

Performance: (Estimated) Max. speed without external stores, 990 mph (1 590 km/h) or Mach 1·5 at 39,370 ft (12 000 m), 720 mph (1 160 km/h) or Mach 0·95 at 1,000 ft (305 m); normal cruise, 595 mph (960 km/h) or Mach 0·9 at 39,370 ft (12 000 m); tactical radius on standard fuel for high-altitude mission, 700 mls (1 125 km); service ceiling, 60,000 ft (18 290 m).

Weights: (Estimated) Max. take-off, 185,000 lb (84 000 kg).

Armament: Free-falling weapons housed internally or (Blinder-B) semi-recessed Kitchen ASM. Remotely-controlled 23-mm cannon in tail barbette.

Status: Believed to have attained operational status with the Soviet Air Forces in 1965. Production believed to be continuing into 1974.

Notes: The Tu-22 is the successor to the subsonic Tu-16 in Soviet medium-bomber formations and with shore-based maritime strike elements of the Soviet Naval Air Arm. The basic version (illustrated above) is dubbed Blinder-A by NATO, the missile-carrying Blinder-B being illustrated on the opposite page. A training version, the Blinder-C, features a raised second cockpit for the instructor. Recent production models of the Tu-22 display a number of modifications, including an extended flight refuelling probe and enlarged engine air intakes, nacelles and exhaust orifices.

TUPOLEV TU-22 (BLINDER)

Dimensions: (Estimated) Span, 91 ft 0 in (27,74 m); length, 133 ft 0 in (40,50 m); height, 17 ft 0 in (5,18 m); wing area, 2,030 sq ft (188,59 m²).

209

TUPOLEV TU-134A (CRUSTY)

Country of Origin: USSR.
Type: Short- to medium-range commercial transport.
Power Plant: Two 14,990 lb (6 800 kg) Soloviev D-30-2 Turbofans.
Performance: Max. cruise, 528 mph (850 km/h) at 32,810 ft (10 000 m); long-range cruise, 466 mph (750 km/h) at 32,810 ft (10 000 m); max. range at long-range cruise with 1 hr reserves and 18,108-lb (8 215-kg) payload, 1,243 mls (2 000 km), with 8,818-lb (4 000-kg) payload, 2,175 mls (3 500 km).
Weights: Operational empty, 63,934 lb (29 000 kg); max. take-off, 103,617 lb (47 000 kg).
Accommodation: Basic flight crew of three and maximum of 80 passengers in four-abreast all-tourist class configuration.
Status: Prototype Tu-134A flown in 1968 and first production deliveries (to *Aeroflot*) mid-1970. Series production continuing at Kharkov at the beginning of 1974.
Notes: The Tu-134A differs from the original Tu-134, which entered *Aeroflot* service in 1966, in having an additional 6 ft 10⅔ in (2,10 m) section inserted in the fuselage immediately forward of the wing to permit two additional rows of passenger seats, and introduces engine thrust reversers. Maximum take-off weight has been increased by 5,512 lb (2 500 kg), maximum payload being raised by 1,025 lb (465 kg), an APU is provided, and radio and navigational equipment have been revised. Route proving trials with the Tu-134A were completed by *Aeroflot* late in 1970, and this airliner was introduced on international routes early in 1971. The shorter-fuselage Tu-134 (illustrated above) serves with Aeroflot CSA, Interflug, LOT, Malev, Bulair, Balkan-Bulgarian and Aviogenex.

TUPOLEV TU-134A (CRUSTY)

Dimensions: Span, 95 ft 2 in (29,00 m); length, 111 ft 0½ in (36,40 m); height, 29 ft 7 in (9,02 m); wing area, 1,370·3 sq ft (127,3 m²).

TUPOLEV TU-144 (CHARGER)

Country of Origin: USSR.

Type: Long-range supersonic commercial transport.

Power Plant: Four 33,100 lb (15 000 kg) dry and 44,000 lb (20 000 kg) reheat Kuznetsov NK-144 turbofans.

Performance: Max. cruise, 1,550 mph (2 500 km/h) or Mach 2·3 at altitudes up to 59,000 ft (18 000 m); subsonic cruise, 614 mph (988 km/h) or Mach 0·93 at 37,730 ft (11 500 m); range (with full payload), 4,000 mls (6 440 km); cruising altitude, 52,500 ft (16 460 m) to 59,000 ft (18 000 m).

Weights: Typical operational empty, 187,395 lb (85 000 kg); max. take-off, 396,830 lb (180 000 kg).

Accommodation: Basic flight crew of three and maximum of up to 140 passengers in single-class arrangement with three-plus-two and two-plus-two seating.

Status: First pre-production aircraft (representative of the production configuration) flown September 1971, and six aircraft of production standard were expected to have flown by the beginning of 1974 when a production rate of one every three weeks was scheduled against an anticipated Aeroflot requirement for approximately 75 aircraft.

Notes: The production-standard Tu-144 described and illustrated on these pages shares little more than a generally similar configuration with the prototype to which this designation was first applied and which flew for the first time on December 31, 1968. The current model has been lengthened by 20 ft 8 in (6,30 m) and the compound delta wing is of 3 ft 9 in (1,15 m) greater span than the ogee wing of the original aircraft; the uprated engines are housed by relocated nacelles, and retractable noseplanes have been added.

212

TUPOLEV TU-144 (CHARGER)

Dimensions: Span, 94 ft 6 in (28,80 m); length, 215 ft 6½ in (65,70 m); height, 42 ft 3 in (12,85 m); wing area, 4,720 sq ft (438 m²).

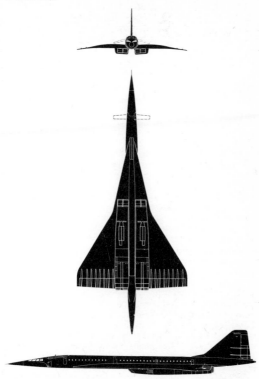

TUPOLEV TU-154 (CARELESS)

Country of Origin: USSR.

Type: Medium- to long-range commercial transport.

Power Plant: Three 20,950 lb (9 500 kg) Kuznetsov NK-8-2 turbofans.

Performance: Max. cruise, 605 mph (975 km/h) at 31,170 ft (9 500 m); long-range cruise, 528 mph (850 km/h) at 37,730 ft (11 500 m); range with standard fuel and reserves of 1 hr plus 6% and max. payload, 2,150 mls (3 460 km) at 560 mph (900 km/h), 2,360 mls (3 800 km) at 528 mph (850 km/h).

Weights: Operational empty, 95,900 lb (43 500 kg); normal take-off, 185,188 lb (84 000 kg); max. take-off, 198,416 lb (90 000 kg).

Accommodation: Basic flight crew of three–four, and alternative arrangements for 158 or 150 economy-class passengers, 150, 146 or 136 tourist-class passengers, or 24 first-class and 104 tourist-class passengers.

Status: First prototype flown October 4, 1968, with first delivery of a production aircraft (to *Aeroflot*) following August 1970, route proving commencing August 1971.

Notes: The Tu-154 entered service on *Aeroflot* routes early 1972, and is intended as a successor to the Tu-104, Il-18 and An-10 on medium- to long-range routes. It can operate from airfields with category B surfaces, including packed earth and gravel. Operators include Aviogenex of Yugoslavia, CSA of Czechoslovakia, Balkan Bulgarian, and Interflug of East Germany. A growth version, referred to as the Tu-154M, is currently under development. This model incorporates additional fuselage sections which will enable 220–240 passengers to be carried, and uprated NK-8 turbofans.

TUPOLEV TU-154 (CARELESS)

Dimensions: Span, 123 ft 2½ in (37,55 m); length, 157 ft 1¾ in (47,90 m); height, 37 ft 4¾ in (11,40 m); wing area, 2,168·92 sq ft (201,45 m²).

VFW-FOKKER VFW 614

Country of Origin: Federal Germany.

Type: Short-range commercial transport.

Power Plant: Two 7,510 (3 410 kg) Rolls-Royce/SNECMA M45H turbofans.

Performance: Max. speed, 457 mph (735 km/h) at 21,000 ft (6 400 m); max. cruise, 457 mph (735 km/h) at 21,000 ft (6 400 m); long-range cruise, 390 mph (627 km/h) at 25,000 ft (7 620 m); range with max. fuel, 1,145 mls (1 845 km), with max. payload, 414 mls (667 km); initial climb rate, 3,410 ft/min (17,3 m/sec).

Weights: Operational empty, 26,896 lb (12 000 kg); max. take-off, 41,006 lb (18 600 kg).

Accommodation: Basic flight crew of two and alternative passenger configurations for 36, 40 or 44 seats in four-abreast rows.

Status: First of three prototypes commenced its flight test programme on June 14, 1971, with second and third following on August 19 and October 10, 1972. First production aircraft scheduled to fly at the end of 1974.

Notes: The VFW 614 is being manufactured as a collaborative venture under the leadership of VFW-Fokker, participants including the Dutch Fokker-VFW concern and the Belgian SABCA and Fairey companies. The VFW 614 is intended as an ultra-short-haul DC-3 replacement, and an unconventional feature is its over-wing engine-pod installation. Emphasis has been placed on flexibility of operation in a wide variety of different environments and with a minimum of maintenance. The VFW 614 is being projected with increased operating weights, max. take-off being raised to 44,000 lb (19 950 kg) which will allow full fuel load with max. payload.

216

VFW-FOKKER VFW 614

Dimensions: Span, 70 ft 6½ in (21,50 m); length, 67 ft 7 in (20,60 m); height, 25 ft 8 in (7,84 m); wing area, 688·89 sq ft (64,00 m²).

VOUGHT A-7E CORSAIR II

Country of Origin: USA.

Type: Single-seat shipboard tactical fighter.

Power Plant: One 15,000 lb (6 804 kg) Allison TF41-A-2 (Rolls-Royce RB. 168-62 Spey) turbofan.

Performance: Max. speed without external stores, 699 mph (1 125 km/h) or Mach 0·92 at sea level, with 12 250-lb (113,4-kg) bombs, 633 mph (1 020 km/h) or Mach 0·87 at sea level; tactical radius with 12 250-lb (113,4-kg) bombs for hi-lo-hi mission at average cruise of 532 mph (856 km/h) with 1 hr on station, 512 mls (825 km); ferry range on internal fuel, 2,775 mls (4 465 km).

Weights: Empty equipped, 17,569 lb (7 969 kg); max. take-off, 42,000+ lb (19 050+ kg).

Armament: One 20-mm M-61A-1 rotary cannon with 1,000 rounds and (for short-range interdiction) maximum ordnance load of 20,000 lb (9 072 kg) distributed between eight external stores stations.

Status: A-7E first flown November 25, 1968, with production deliveries to US Navy following mid-1969. First 67 delivered with Pratt & Whitney TF30-P-8 turbofan. Planned procurement totals 706 aircraft, of which 488 had been funded to the beginning of 1974.

Notes: A-7E is the shipboard equivalent of the USAF's A-7D (see 1970 edition). Preceded into service by A-7A (199 built) and A-7B (196 built) with 11,350 lb (5 150 kg) TF30-P-6 and 12,200 lb (5 534 kg) TF30-P-8 respectively. The A-7G was a proposed version for the Swiss Air Force with an uprated TF41-A-3 turbofan, and a company-funded tandem two-seat version (see 1973 edition) is designated YA-7H.

VOUGHT A-7E CORSAIR II

Dimensions: Span, 38 ft 8¾ in (11,80 m); length, 46 ft 1½ in (14,06 m); height, 16 ft 0¾ in (4,90 m); wing area, 375 sq ft (34,83 m²).

WSK-MIELEC M-15

Country of Origin: Poland.

Type: Agricultural biplane.

Power Plant: One 3,307 lb (1 500 kg) Ivchenko AI-25 turbofan.

Performance: (Estimated) Max. cruise, 168 mph (270 km/h); normal operating speeds, 87–112 mph (140–180 km/h); max. range, 620 mls (1 000 km) at 9,840 ft (3 000 m); initial climb, 964 ft/min (4,9 m/sec); max. climb, 1,673 ft/min (8,5 m/sec).

Weights: Empty, 5,291 lb (2 400 kg); max. take-off, 11,684 lb (5 300 kg).

Status: First of two prototypes flown July 1973 with planned production deliveries commencing (to the Soviet Union) late 1974.

Notes: The world's first turbojet-driven biplane, the M-15 is an agricultural aircraft of radical concept evolved by a joint Polish-Soviet design team. The cockpit provides accommodation for a single pilot, but provision is made in the centre section of the fuselage pod for transportation of an engineer. Twin chemical containers are mounted between the upper and lower wings and these have a total capacity of 638 Imp gal (2 900 l) or 4,850 lb (2 200 kg) of liquid or powdered materials. Air is tapped from the turbofan's low-pressure compressor to drive the agricultural equipment in the tail of the fuselage pod and in the rear portion of the lower wing. A project exists for a utility transport version with accommodation for two passengers in each of two modified interwing pods.

WSK-MIELEC M-15

Dimensions: Span, 72 ft 2⅛ in (22,00 m); length, 41 ft 1⅓ in (12,53 m); height, 17 ft 0¼ in (5,20 m); wing area, 723·33 sq ft (67,20 m²).

YAKOVLEV YAK-40 (CODLING)

Country of Origin: USSR.

Type: Short-range commercial feederliner.

Power Plant: Three 3,307 lb (1 500 kg) Ivchenko AI-25 turbofans.

Performance: Max. speed, 373 mph (600 km/h) at sea level, 466 mph (750 km/h) at 17,000 ft (5 180 m); max. cruise, 342 mph (550 km/h) at 19,685 ft (6 000 m); econ. cruise, 310 mph (500 km/h) at 32,810 ft (10 000 m); range with 5,070-lb (2 300-kg) payload at econ. cruise, 620 mls (1 000 km), with 3,140-lb (1 425-kg) payload and max. fuel, 920 mls (1 480 km); initial climb, 2,000 ft/min (10,16 m/sec); service ceiling at max. loaded weight, 38,715 ft (11 800 m).

Weights: Empty equipped, 19,865–21,715 lb (9 010– 9 850 kg); normal take-off, 27,250–34,170 lb (12 360– 15 500 kg); max. take-off, 36,375 lb (16 500 kg).

Accommodation: Flight crew of two, and alternative arrangements for 27 or 34 passengers in three-abreast rows. High-density arrangement for 40 passengers in four-abreast rows, and business executive configuration for 8–10 passengers.

Status: First of five prototypes flown October 21, 1966, and first production deliveries (to *Aeroflot*) mid-1968. Some 400 delivered by beginning of 1973.

Notes: A thrust reverser introduced as standard on centre engine during 1971 when more powerful version with three 3,858 lb (1 750 kg) AI-25T turbofans and increased fuel capacity announced for 1974 delivery as the Yak-40V. The uprated power plant is already installed in Yak-40s serving in the liaison role with the Soviet Air Forces.

YAKOVLEV YAK-40 (CODLING)

Dimensions: Span, 82 ft 0¼ in (25,00 m); length, 66 ft 9½ in (20,36 m); height, 21 ft 4 in (6,50 m); wing area, 753·473 sq ft (70 m²).

AÉROSPATIALE SA 315B LAMA

Country of Origin: France.
Type: Five-seat light utility helicopter.
Power Plant: One 870 shp (derated to 550 shp) Turboméca Artouste IIIB turboshaft.
Performance: Max. speed, 130 mph (210 km/h) at sea level; max. cruise, 119 mph (192 km/h), with slung load, 75 mph (120 km/h); max. inclined climb rate, 1,319 ft/min (6,7 m/sec); hovering ceiling (in ground effect), 8,530 ft (2 600 m), (out of ground effect), 1,312 ft (400 m); range (at 3,858 lb/1 750 kg), 317 mls (510 km) at sea level, 373 mls (600 km) at 9,840 ft (3 000 m).
Weights: Empty, 2,193 lb (995 kg); max. take-off, 4,850 lb (2 200 kg).
Dimensions: Rotor diam, 36 ft $1\frac{3}{4}$ in (11,02 m); fuselage length, 33 ft 8 in (10,26 m).
Notes: Flown for the first time on March 17, 1969, the Lama combines features of the SA 318C Alouette II (see 1973 edition) and the SA 319A Alouette III (see opposite), having the airframe of the former (with some reinforcement) and the dynamic components of the latter. Developed primarily to meet the requirements of the Indian armed forces, the Lama is manufactured under licence by Hindustan Aeronautics as the Cheetah. The Lama can transport an external load of 2,204 lb (1 000 kg) at an altitude of more than 8,200 ft (2 500 m).

AÉROSPATIALE SA 319A ALOUETTE III

Country of Origin: France.

Type: Seven-seat light utility helicopter.

Power Plant: One 789 shp Turboméca Astazou XIV turboshaft.

Performance: Max. speed, 137 mph (220 km/h) at sea level; max. cruise, 122 mph (197 km/h); max. inclined climb, 853 ft/min (4,32 m/sec); hovering ceiling (in ground effect), 5,740 ft (1 750 m); range with six passengers, 375 mls (605 km).

Weights: Empty, 2,403 lb (1 090 kg); max. take-off, 4,960 lb (2 250 kg).

Dimensions: Rotor diam, 36 ft $1\frac{3}{4}$ in (11,02 m); fuselage length, 32 ft $10\frac{3}{4}$ in (10,03 m).

Notes: The SA 319 is an Astazou-powered derivative of the Artouste-powered SA 316 Alouette III. All Alouette IIIs built prior to 1970 had the Artouste turboshaft and are now designated SA 316A, the 1970 production model with the Artouste IIIB of 858 shp derated to 543 shp being the SA 316B, and the 1972 model with the Artouste IIID being the SA 316C. The last-mentioned version is manufactured in parallel with the SA 319A, deliveries of which began late in 1970, and the SA 319B with the Astazou XVI was introduced in 1971. Some 1,100 Alouette IIIs had been ordered by the beginning of 1974, and licence production was being under-taken in India, Switzerland, and Rumania.

AÉROSPATIALE SA 330 PUMA

Country of Origin: France.
Type: Medium transport helicopter.
Power Plant: Two 1,320 shp Turboméca Turmo III C4 turboshafts.
Performance: Max. Speed, 174 mph (280 km/h) at sea level; max. cruise, 165 mph (265 km/h); max. inclined climb, 1,400 ft/min (7,1 m/sec); hovering ceiling (in ground effect), 9,186 ft (2 800 m), (out of ground effect), 6,233 ft (1 900 m); max. range, 390 mls (630 km).
Weights: Empty, 7,561 lb (3 430 kg); max. take-off, 14,110 (6 400 kg).
Dimensions: Rotor diam, 49 ft 2½ on (15,00 m), fuselage length, 46 ft 1½ in (14,06 m).
Notes: The Puma is being built under a joint production agreement between Aérospatiale and Westland, the first to be assembled by the latter concern flying on November 25, 1970. The Puma can accommodate 16–20 troops or up to 5,511 lb (2 500 kg) of cargo, and 40 are being delivered to the RAF for the assault role, 130 having been ordered by French Army Aviation. The Puma has been supplied to the Portuguese, South African, Zaïre Rep., Abu Dhabian, Algerian, and Ivory Coast air arms, and a commercial version, the SA 330F with 1,385 shp Turmo IVA turboshafts, obtained FAA Type Approval in 1971, this carrying 15–17 passengers over 217 mls (350 km).

AÉROSPATIALE SA 341 GAZELLE

Country of Origin: France.
Type: Five-seat light utility helicopter.
Power Plant: One 592 shp Turboméca Astazou IIIN turbo-shaft.
Performance: Max. speed, 165 mph (265 km/h) at sea level; max. cruise, 149 mph (240 km/h); max. inclined climb rate, 1,214 ft/min (6,16 m/sec); hovering ceiling (in ground effect), 10,170 ft (3 100 m), (out of ground effect), 8,530 ft (2 600 m); max. range, 403 mls (650 km).
Weights: Empty, 1,873 lb (850 kg); max. take-off, 3,747 lb (1 700 kg).
Dimensions: Rotor diam, 34 ft 5½ in (10,50 m); fuselage length, 31 ft 2¾ in (9,52 m).
Notes: Intended as a successor to the Alouette II, the Gazelle is being built under a joint production agreement between Aérospatiale and Westland. Two prototypes and four pre-production Gazelles were flown, and the first production example flew on August 6, 1971. The Gazelle is to be operated in the LOH (Light Observation Helicopter) role by both the French (SA 341F) and British armed forces (SA 341B for the Army, SA 341C for the Navy and SA 341D for the RAF), and it is anticipated that these will respectively purchase some 170 and 250 Gazelles during the first half of the decade. Licence production is being undertaken in Yugoslavia and deliveries commenced late 1973.

AÉROSPATIALE SA 360

Country of Origin: France.
Type: Multi-purpose and transport helicopter.
Power Plant: One 1,025 shp (derated to 878 shp) Turbo-méca Astazou XVIIIA turboshaft.
Performance: Max. cruise, 171 mph (275 km/h); econ. cruise, 143 mph (230 km/h); inclined climb rate (at 5,500 lb/2 500 kg), 1,476 ft/min (7,5 m/sec); hovering ceiling (in ground effect), 15,584 ft (4 750 m), (out of ground effect), 14,107 ft (4 300 m); range (with 2,204-lb/1 000-kg payload), 62 mls (100 km), (with 1,323-lb/600-kg payload), 466 mls (750 km).
Weights: Empty equipped, 2,976 lb (1 350 kg); max. take-off, 5,952 lb (2 700 kg).
Dimensions: Rotor diam, 37 ft 8¾ in (11,50 m); fuselage length, 36 ft 4 in (11,08 m).
Notes: Intended as a successor to the Alouette III, the SA 360 utilises a semi-rigid four-blade rotor and a ducted 11-blade tail rotor. The two prototypes made their initial flights on June 2, 1972, and January 29, 1973, respectively, and the first production example is scheduled for completion mid-1975. A twin-engined derivative, the SA 365, is under development with two 681 shp Turboméca Arriel free tur-bines and an optional retractable undercarriage. A projected variant is the SA 366 with two 582 shp Avco Lycoming LTS 101 turboshafts.

AGUSTA A 109C HIRUNDO

Country of Origin: Italy.
Type: Eight-seat utility helicopter.
Power Plant: Two 400 shp Allison 250-C20 turboshafts.
Performance: (At 4,850 lb/2 200 kg) Max. speed, 169 mph (272 km/h) at sea level; econ. cruise, 139 mph (223 km/h) at sea level; max. inclined climb, 2,067 ft/min (10,5 m/sec); hovering ceiling (in ground effect), 11,810 ft (3 600 m), (out of ground effect), 9,190 ft (2 800 m); max. range, 457 mls (735 km) at 6,560 ft (2 000 m).
Weights: Empty, 2,645 lb (1 200 kg); max. take-off, 5,291 lb (2 400 kg).
Dimensions: Rotor diam, 36 ft 1 in (11,00 m); fuselage length, 36 ft 7 in (11,14 m).
Notes: The first of four Hirundo (Swallow) prototypes flew on August 4, 1971. This was lost as a result of resonance problems, flight trials being resumed with the second and third prototypes early 1973. The first production examples are scheduled to be delivered during 1974. The Hirundo is intended to fit between the licence-built Bell 206 JetRanger and Bell 212 in the Agusta helicopter range, and carries a pilot and seven passengers in its basic form. It is also suitable for the ambulance role, accommodating two casualty stretchers and two medical attendants when the forward cabin bulkhead is removed, and for freight carrying the forward row of passenger seats may be removed.

BELL MODEL 205A (IROQUOIS)

Country of Origin: USA.

Type: Fifteen-seat utility helicopter.

Power Plant: One 1,400 shp Lycoming T5313A turboshaft.

Performance: (At 9,500 lb/4 309 kg) Max. speed, 127 mph (204 km/h) at sea level; max. cruise, 111 mph (179 km/h) at 8,000 ft (2 440 m); max. inclined climb, 1,680 ft/min (8,53 m/sec); hovering ceiling (in ground effect), 10,400 ft (3 170 m), (out of ground effect), 6,000 ft (1 830 m); range, 344 mls (553 km) at 8,000 ft (2 440 m).

Weights: Empty equipped, 5,082 lb (2 305 kg); normal take-off, 9,500 lb (4 309 kg).

Dimensions: Rotor diam, 48 ft 0 in (14,63 m); fuselage length, 41 ft 6 in (12,65 m).

Notes: The Model 205A is basically similar to the Model 204B (see 1973 edition) but introduces a longer fuselage with increased cabin space. It is produced under licence in Italy by Agusta as the AB 205, and is assembled under licence in Formosa (Taiwan). The initial version for the US Army, the UH-1D, had a 1,100 shp T53-L-11 turboshaft. This model was manufactured under licence in Federal Germany. The UH-1D has been succeeded in production for the US Army by the UH-1H with a 1,400 shp T53-L-13 turboshaft, and a similar helicopter for the Mobile Command of the Canadian Armed Forces is designated CUH-1H. A progressive development is the Model 214 (see page 235).

BELL MODEL 206B JETRANGER II

Country of Origin: USA.

Type: Five-seat light utility helicopter.

Power Plant: One 400 shp Allison 250-C20 turboshaft.

Performance: (At 3,000 lb/1 361 kg) Max. cruise, 136 mph (219 km/h) at sea level, 142 mph (228 km/h) at 5,000 ft (1 524 m); hovering ceiling (in ground effect), 13,200 ft (4 023 m), (out of ground effect), 8,700 ft (2 652 m); max. inclined climb, 1,540 ft/min (7,82 m/sec); max. range, 436 mls (702 km) at 10,000 ft (3 048 m).

Weights: Empty, 1,455 lb (660 kg); max. take-off, 3,000 lb (1 360 kg).

Dimensions: Rotor diam, 33 ft 4 in (10,16 m); fuselage length, 31 ft 2 in (9,50 m).

Notes: The JetRanger is manufactured in both commercial and military versions, and the current production variant, the Model 206B JetRanger II, differs from the Model 206A Jet-Ranger in having an uprated turboshaft. A light observation version for the US Army is known as the OH-58A Kiowa, and a training version for the US Navy is known as the TH-57A SeaRanger. An Australian-built version of the Model 206B is being delivered to the Australian Army, and this helicopter is also built in Italy by Agusta as the AB 206B-1. The OH-58A Kiowa has a larger main rotor of 35 ft 4 in (10,77 m) diameter and a fuselage of 32 ft 3½ in (9,84 m) length.

BELL MODEL 206L LONG RANGER

Country of Origin: USA.
Type: Seven-seat light utility helicopter.
Power Plant: One 420 shp Allison 250-C20B turboshaft.
Performance: (At 3,900 lb/1 769 kg) Max. speed, 144 mph (232 km/h); cruise, 136 mph (229 km/h) at sea level; hovering ceiling (in ground effect), 8,200 ft (2 499 m), (out of ground effect), 2,000 ft (610 m); range, 390 mls (628 km) at sea level, 430 mls (692 km) at 5,000 ft (1 524 m).
Weights: Empty, 1,861 lb (844 kg); max. take-off, 3,900 lb (1 769 kg).
Dimensions: Rotor diam. 37 ft 0 in (11,28 m); fuselage length, 33 ft 3 in (10,13 m).
Notes: The Model 206L Long Ranger is a stretched and more powerful version of the Model 206B JetRanger II, with a longer fuselage, increased fuel capacity, an uprated engine and a larger rotor. The Long Ranger is to be manufactured in parallel with the JetRanger II with initial customer deliveries scheduled for early 1975, prototype testing having been initiated during the course of 1973. The Long Ranger will be available with emergency flotation gear and with a 2,000-lb (907-kg) capacity cargo hook. Cabin volume is 83 cu ft (2,35 m³) as compared with the 49 cu ft (1,39 m³) of the JetRanger II (see page 231). By 1974, more than 1,000 commercial and 2,000 military examples of the basic JetRanger series had been delivered.

BELL MODEL 209 HUEYCOBRA

Country of Origin: USA.

Type: Two-seat attack helicopter.

Power Plant: One 1,800 shp Pratt & Whitney (UACL) T400-CP-400 coupled turboshaft.

Performance: Max. speed, 207 mph (333 km/h) at sea level; max. range (without reserves, 359 mls (577 km); max. inclined climb, 1,090 ft/min (5,54 m/sec); hovering ceiling (in ground effect), 12,450 ft (3 794 m).

Weights: Operational (including crew), 6,816 lb (3 091 kg); max. take-off, 10,000 lb (4 535 kg).

Dimensions: Rotor diam, 44 ft 0 in (13,41 m); fuselage length, 44 ft 7 in (13,59 m).

Notes: The version of the Model 209 HueyCobra described above is employed by the US Marine Corps as the AH-1J SeaCobra, differing from the US Army's AH-1G primarily in having a "Twin Pac" power plant. Eighty-nine AH-1Js are being procured by the USMC from funding up to and including Fiscal 1974 with procurement of a further 35 planned, and 202 examples are being supplied to Iran with deliveries commencing April 1974. By comparison with the AH-1G, the AH-1J has an improved armament system embodying a three-barrelled 20-mm XM-197 cannon in a chin turret. Four external stores attachment points under the stub-wings can carry a variety of ordnance loads, including Minigun pods and rocket packs.

233

BELL MODEL 212 TWIN TWO-TWELVE

Country of Origin: USA.

Type: Fifteen-seat utility helicopter.

Power Plant: One 1,800 shp Pratt & Whitney PT6T-3 coupled turboshaft.

Performance: Max. speed, 121 mph (194 km/h) at sea level; max. inclined climb at 10,000 lb (4 535 kg), 1,460 ft/min (7,4 m/sec); hovering ceiling (in ground effect), 17,100 ft (5 212 m), (out of ground effect), 9,900 ft (3 020 m); max. range, 296 mls (476 km) at sea level.

Weights: Empty, 5,500 lb (2 495 kg); max. take-off, 10,000 lb (4 535 kg).

Dimensions: Rotor diam, 48 ft 2½ in (14,69 m); fuselage length, 42 ft 10¾ in (13,07 m).

Notes: The Model 212 is based on the Model 205 (see page 230) from which it differs primarily in having a twin-engined power plant (two turboshaft engines coupled to a combining gearbox with a single output shaft), and both commercial and military versions are being produced. A model for the Canadian Armed Forces is designated CUH-1N, and an essentially similar variant of the Model 212, the UH-1N, is being supplied to the USAF, the USN, and the USMC. All versions of the Model 212 can carry an external load of 4,400 lb (1 814 kg), and can maintain cruise performance on one engine component at maximum gross weight.

BELL MODEL 214

Country of Origin: USA.

Type: Sixteen-seat utility helicopter.

Power Plant: One 2,930 shp Avco Lycoming T55-L-7C turboshaft.

Performance: Max. speed, 190 mph (305 km/h) at sea level; max. cruise (at gross weight of 13,000 lb/5 897 kg), 150 mph (241 km/h); range, 300 mls (483 km).

Weights: Normal max. take-off, 13,000 lb (5 897 kg), (with slung load), 15,000 lb (6 804 kg).

Dimensions: Rotor diam, 50 ft 0 in (15,20 m).

Notes: Development of the Model 214, originally known as the HueyPlus, was initiated in 1970 as a progressive development of the Model 205 (UH-1H). Utilising an essentially similar airframe with strengthened main beams, pylon structure and aft fuselage, and the main rotor and tail rotor drive systems of the Model 309 KingCobra (see 1973 edition) coupled with the Lycoming T55-L-7C turboshaft installed in the second KingCobra, this utility helicopter is being developed for military use as the Model 214A and will be certificated for commercial use as the Model 214B (Avco Lycoming LTC4B-8D). First flight of the Model 214A was scheduled for early 1974, and first deliveries against orders from the Iranian Government for 287 helicopters of this type are scheduled for February 1975, at which time the Model 214B will be certificated.

BOEING VERTOL MODEL 114

Country of Origin: USA.

Type: Medium transport helicopter.

Power Plant: (CH-47C) Two 3,750 shp Lycoming T55-L-11 turboshafts.

Performance: (CH-47C at 33,000 lb/14 969 kg) Max. speed, 190 mph (306 km/h) at sea level; average cruise, 158 mph (254 km/h); max. inclined climb, 2,880 ft/min (14,63 m/sec); hovering ceiling (out of ground effect), 14,750 ft (4 495 m); mission radius, 115 mls (185 km).

Weights: Empty, 20,378 lb (9 243); max. take-off, 46,000 lb (20 865 kg).

Dimensions: Rotor diam (each), 60 ft 0 in (18,29 m); fuselage length, 51 ft 0 in (15,54 m).

Notes: The Model 114 is the standard medium transport helicopter of the US Army, and is operated by that service under the designation CH-47 Chinook. The initial production model, the CH-47A, was powered by 2,200 shp T55-L-5 or 2,650 shp T55-L-7 turboshafts. This was succeeded by the CH-47B with 2,850 shp T55-L-7C engines, redesigned rotor blades and other modifications, and this, in turn, gave place to the current CH-47C with more powerful engines, strengthened transmissions, and increased fuel capacity. This model is manufactured in Italy by Elicotteri Meriodionali, orders calling for 26 for the Italian Army and 16 for the Iranian Army.

236

BOEING VERTOL MODEL 179

Country of Origin: USA.
Type: Tactical transport helicopter.
Power Plant: Two (approx.) 1,500 shp General Electric T700-GE-700 turboshafts.
Performance: No details available for publication.
Weights: Max. take-off, 15,000 lb (6 804 kg) category.
Dimensions: No details available for publication.
Notes: The Model 179 is a finalist in the US Army's UTTAS (Utility Tactical Transport Aircraft System) contest under the designation YUH-61A, the other being the Sikorsky YUH-60-A (see page 249). The UTTAS requirement is for a successor for the Bell UH-1H Iroquois (see page 230) in the troop transportation, medical evacuation and the logistics support roles from the late 'seventies, and one static test example and three flying prototypes of the YUH-61A have been ordered, the schedule calling for the flying prototypes to commence their test programme in November and December 1974 and January 1975 respectively. After a year of manufacturer's trials, the YUH-61A will commence official US Army trials and competitive evaluation against the YUH-60A, leading to a production award for one design in March 1977 with production deliveries commencing mid-1978. The YUH-61A will accommodate 11 fully-equipped troops in addition to a crew of three, and a company-owned example is also being built to develop commercial sales.

HUGHES MODEL 500

Country of Origin: USA.

Type: Six-seat light utility helicopter.

Power Plant: One 317 shp Allison 250-C18A turboshaft.

Performance: Max. speed, 152 mph (244 km/h) at 1,000 ft (305 m); range cruise, 138 mph (222 km/h) at sea level; max. inclined climb, 1,700 ft/min (8,64 m/sec); hovering ceiling (in ground effect), 8,200 ft (2 500 m), (out of ground effect), 5,300 ft (1 615 m); max. range, 377 mls (589 km) at 4,000 ft (1 220 m).

Weights: Empty, 1,086 lb (492 kg); max. take-off, 2,550 lb (1 157 kg).

Dimensions: Rotor diam, 26 ft 4 in (8,03 m); fuselage length, 23 ft 0 in (7,01 m).

Notes: The Model 500 (also known by the engineering designation Model 369) is being manufactured for both commercial and foreign military use, the military configuration being known as the Model 500M. Both Models 500 and 500M have been assembled in Italy by Nardi which began licence manufacture during 1971, and licence manufacture is also being undertaken by Kawasaki in Japan. The current Model 500 is essentially similar to the OH-6A Cayuse light observation helicopter for the US Army, but its turboshaft is only derated to 278 shp (as compared with 252 shp for the Allison T63-A-5A of the OH-6A), and internal volume and fuel capacity are increased.

KAMAN HH-2 SEASPRITE

Country of Origin: USA.
Type: All-weather search and rescue helicopter.
Power Plant: Two 1,250 shp General Electric T58-GE-8B turboshafts.
Performace: (HH-2D) Max. speed, 168 mph (270 km/h) at sea level; normal cruise, 152 mph (245 km/h); max. inclined climb, 2,540 ft/min (12,9 m/sec); hovering ceiling (in ground effect), 16,900 ft (5 150 m), (out of ground effect), 14,100 ft (4 300 m); max. range, 425 mls (685 km).
Weights: (HH-2D) Empty, 7,500 lb (3 401 kg); normal take-off, 10,187 lb (4 620 kg); max. overload, 12,500 lb (5 670 kg).
Dimensions: Rotor diam, 44 ft 0 in (13,41 m); fuselage length, 37 ft 8 in (11,48 m).
Notes: The HH-2C and HH-2D are specialised search and rescue conversions of the single-engined UH-2A and -2B multi-role versions of the Seasprite (see 1966 edition), and, like the UH-2C (see 1969 edition), are modified to twin-engined configuration. The HH-2C is an armed and armoured model with a chin-mounted Minigun barbette and waist-mounted machine guns, and the HH-2D is similar but lacks armour and armament. The HH-2D differs from the UH-2C in having a four-bladed tail rotor, dual main-wheels, and uprated transmission, and the SH-2F (illustrated) is an adaptation for anti-submarine warfare and missile defence.

239

KAMOV KA-25 (HORMONE A)

Country of Origin: USSR.
Type: Shipboard anti-submarine warfare helicopter.
Power Plant: Two 900 shp Glushenkov GTD-3 turboshafts.
Performance: (Estimated) Max. speed, 130 mph (209 km/h); normal cruise, 120 mph (193 km/h); max. range, 400 mls (644 km); service ceiling, 11,000 ft (3 353 m).
Weights: (Estimated) Empty, 10,500 lb (4 765 kg); max. take-off, 16,500 lb (7 484 kg).
Dimensions: Rotor diam (each), 51 ft $7\frac{1}{2}$ in (15,74 m); approx. fuselage length, 35 ft 6 in (10,82 m).
Notes: Possessing a basically similar airframe to that of the Ka-25K (see 1973 edition) and employing a similar self-contained assembly comprising rotors, transmission, engines and auxiliaries, the Ka-25 serves with the Soviet Navy primarily in the ASW role but is also employed in the utility and transport roles. The ASW Ka-25 serves aboard the helicopter cruisers *Moskva* and *Leningrad* as well as with shore-based units. A search radar installation is mounted in a nose radome, but other sensor housings and antennae differ widely from helicopter to helicopter. There is no evidence that externally-mounted weapons may be carried. Each landing wheel is surrounded by an inflatable pontoon surmounted by inflation bottles. Sufficient capacity is available to accommodate up to a dozen personnel. The commercial Ka-25K can be employed in the flying crane role.

MBB BO 105

Country of Origin: Federal Germany.
Type: Five/six-seat light utility helicopter.
Power Plant: Two 400 shp Allison 250-C20 turboshafts.
Performance: Max. speed, 155 mph (250 km/h) at sea level; max. cruise, 138 mph (222 km/h); max. inclined climb, 1,870 ft/min (9,5 m/sec); hovering ceiling (in ground effect), 7,610 ft (2 320 m), (out of ground effect), 5,085 ft (1 550 m); normal range, 388 mls (625 km) at 5,000 ft (1 525 m).
Weights: Empty, 2,360 lb (1 070 kg); normal take-off, 4,630 lb (2 100 kg); max. take-off, 5,070 lb (2 300 kg).
Dimensions: Rotor diam, 32 ft 1¾ in (9,80 m); fuselage length, 28 ft 0½ in (8,55 m).
Notes: The BO 105 features a rigid unarticulated main rotor with folding glass-fibre reinforced plastic blades, and the first prototype (with a conventional rotor) was tested in 1966, three prototypes being followed by four pre-production examples, and production deliveries commencing during 1971. The German armed forces have acquired examples for evaluation. The third prototype was powered by 375 shp MTU 6022 turboshafts, but the production model has standardised on the Allison 250. Production is undertaken by the Siebelwerke-ATG subsidiary of MBB and the 100th BO 105 was flown mid-1973. A seven-seat derivative, the BO 106, was flown on September 25, 1973.

MIL MI-8 (HIP)

Country of Origin: USSR.
Type: General-purpose transport helicopter.
Power Plant: Two 1,500 shp Izotov TB-2-117A turboshafts.
Performance: (At 24,470 lb/11 100 kg) Max. speed, 155 mph (250 km/h); max. cruise, 140 mph (225 km/h); hovering ceiling (in ground effect), 5,900 ft (1 800 m), (out of ground effect), 2,625 ft (800 m); service ceiling, 14,760 ft (4 500 m); range with 6,615 lb (3 000 kg) of freight, 264 mls (425 km).
Weights: Empty (cargo), 15,787 lb (7 171 kg), (passenger), 16,352 lb (7 417 kg); normal take-off, 24,470 lb (11 100 kg); max. take-off (for VTO), 26,455 lb (12 000 kg).
Dimensions: Rotor diam, 69 ft 10¼ in (21,29 m); fuselage length, 59 ft 7⅓ in (18,17 m).
Notes: The Mi-8 has been in continuous production since 1964 for both civil and military tasks. The standard commercial passenger version has a basic flight crew of two or three and 28 four-abreast seats, and the aeromedical version accommodates 12 casualty stretchers and a medical attendant. As a freighter the Mi-8 will carry up to 8,818 lb (4 000 kg) of cargo, and military tasks include assault transport, search and rescue, and anti-submarine warfare. The Mi-8 is now operated by several Warsaw Pact air forces, serving primarily in the support transport role, and has been exported to numerous countries, including Finland, Pakistan and Egypt.

MIL MI-12 (HOMER)

Country of Origin: USSR.
Type: Heavy transport helicopter.
Power Plant: Four 6,500 shp Soloviev D-25VF turboshafts.
Performance: Max. speed, 161 mph (260 km/h); cruise, 149 mph (240 km/h); range with max. payload of 78,000 lb (35 380 kg), 310 mls (500 km); service ceiling, 11,500 ft (3 500 m).
Weights: Normal take-off, 213,848 lb (97 000 kg); max. take-off, 231,485 lb (105 000 kg).
Dimensions: Rotor diam (each), 114 ft 9½ in (35,00 m); fuselage length, 121 ft 4 in (37,00 m).
Notes: First flown in the autumn of 1968 and currently the world's largest helicopter, the Mi-12 carries a crew of six of which the pilot, co-pilot, flight engineer and electrician are accommodated on the lower flight deck with the navigator and radio-operator on the upper deck. The Mi-12 employs the dynamic components of the Mi-6 (see 1973 edition), being in effect two Mi-6 power units, main transmissions and main rotors mounted side-by-side at the tips of braced wings, the overall width with the rotors turning being 219 ft 9 in (67,00 m). The Mi-12 was evidently designed to carry loads compatible with those carried by the fixed-wing An-22 transport, and three prototypes have been built. Production is expected to commence during the course of 1974 for both the Soviet Air Forces and *Aeroflot*.

SIKORSKY S-61A

Country of Origin: USA.
Type: Amphibious transport and rescue helicopter.
Power Plant: (S-61A-4) Two 1,500 shp General Electric T58-GE-5 turboshafts.
Performance: (At 20,500 lb/9 300 kg) Max. speed, 153 mph (248 km/h); range cruise, 126 mph (203 km/h); max. inclined climb, 2,200 ft/min (11,17 m/sec); hovering ceiling. (in ground effect), 8,600 ft (2 820 m); range with max. fuel and 10 % reserves, 525 mls (845 km).
Weights: Empty, 9,763 lb (4 428 kg); normal take-off, 20,500 lb (9 300 kg); max., 21,500 lb (9 750 kg).
Dimensions: Rotor diam, 62 ft 0 in (18,90 m); fuselage length, 54 ft 9 in (16,69 m).
Notes: A transport equivalent of the S-61D (see page 245) with sonar, weapons, and automatic blade folding deleted, and a cargo floor inserted, the S-61A is used by the USAF for missile site support as the CH-3B, this having 1,250 shp T58-GE-8Bs and accommodation for 26 troops or 15 stretchers. Eight similarly-powered S-61A-1s supplied to Denmark for the rescue task were supplemented in 1970 by a ninth machine, and 10 T58-GE-5-powered S-61A-4s equipped to carry 31 combat troops and supplied to Malaysia were supplemented during 1971 by six further S-61A-4s. The S-61L and S-61N (see 1967 edition) are non-amphibious and amphibious commercial versions.

244

SIKORSKY S-61D (SEA KING)

Country of Origin: USA.

Type: Amphibious anti-submarine helicopter.

Power Plant: Two 1,500 shp General Electric T58-GE-10 turboshafts.

Performance: Max. speed, 172 mph (277 km/h) at sea level; inclined climb, 2,200 ft/min (11,2 m/sec); hovering ceiling (out of ground effect), 8,200 ft (2 500 m); range (with 10% reserves), 622 mls (1 000 km).

Weights: Empty equipped, 12,087 lb (5 481 kg); max. take-off, 20,500 lb (9 297 kg).

Dimensions: Rotor diam, 62 ft 0 in (18,90 m); fuselage length, 54 ft 9 in (16,69 m).

Notes: A more powerful derivative of the S-61B, the S-61D serves with the US Navy as the SH-3D, 74 helicopters of this type following on production of 255 SH-3As (S-61Bs) for the ASW role. Licence manufacture of the S-61D (with 1,500 shp Rolls-Royce Gnome turboshafts) is undertaken in the UK by Westland as the Sea King HAS Mk. 1, 56 being delivered to the Royal Navy. Deliveries of the improved Sea King Mk. 50 for the Royal Australian Navy will commence during 1974, and production is being undertaken of a tactical transport version, the Commando (see page 250). Licence manufacture of the S-61D is also being undertaken in Italy by Agusta for the Italian and Iranian navies. The SH-3G and SH-3H are upgraded conversions of the SH-3A.

SIKORSKY S-61R

Country of Origin: USA.

Type: Amphibious transport and rescue helicopter.

Power Plant: (CH-3E) Two 1,500 shp General Electric T58-GE-5 turboshafts.

Performance: (CH-3E at 21,247 lb/9 635 kg) Max. speed, 162 mph (261 km/h) at sea level; range cruise, 144 mph (232 km/h); max. inclined climb, 1,310 ft/min (6,6 m/sec); hovering ceiling (in ground effect), 4,100 ft (1 250 m); range with 10% reserves, 465 mls (748 km).

Weights: (CH-3E) Empty, 13,255 lb (6 010 kg); normal take-off, 21,247 lb (9 635 kg); max. take-off, 22,050 lb (10 000 kg).

Dimensions: Rotor diam, 62 ft 0 in (18,90 m); fuselage length, 57 ft 3 in (17,45 m).

Notes: Although based on the S-61A, the S-61R embodies numerous design changes, including a rear ramp and a tricycle-type undercarriage. Initial model for the USAF was the CH-3C with 1,300 shp T58-GE-1 turboshafts, but this was subsequently updated to CH-3E standards. The CH-3E can accommodate 25–30 troops or 5,000 lb (2 270 kg) of cargo, and may be fitted with a TAT-102 barbette on each sponson mounting a 7,62-mm Minigun. The HH-3E is a USAF rescue version with armour, self-sealing tanks, and refuelling probe, and the HH-3F Pelican (illustrated) is a US Coast Guard search and rescue model.

SIKORSKY S-64 SKYCRANE

Country of Origin: USA.

Type: Heavy flying-crane helicopter.

Power Plant: Two 4,500 shp Pratt & Whitney T73-P-1 turboshafts.

Performance: (CH-54A at 38,000 lb/17 237 kg) Max. speed, 127 mph (204 km/h) at sea level; max. cruise, 109 mph (175 km/h); max. inclined climb, 1,700 ft/min (8,64 m/sec); hovering ceiling (in ground effect), 10,600 ft (3 230 m), (out of ground effect), 6,900 ft (2 100 m); range, 253 mls (407 km).

Weights: (CH-54A) Empty, 19,234 lb (8 724 kg); max. take-off, 42,000 lb (19 050 kg).

Dimensions: Rotor diam, 72 ft 0 in (21,95 m); fuselage length, 70 ft 3 in (21,41 m).

Notes: The S-64A serves with the US Army as the CH-54A Tarhe in the heavy lift role, and may be fitted with a 15,000-lb (6 800-kg) hoist or an all-purpose pod which can accommodate 45 troops or 24 casualty stretchers. The commercial equivalent of the CH-54A is designated S-64E. A developed version, the CH-54B powered by T73-P-700 turboshafts of 4,800 shp, was flown on June 30, 1969, other changes including dual mainwheels and an increase in max. take-off to 47,000 lb (21 319 kg). The CH-54B also features a new gearbox and high-lift rotor blades, the civil equivalent being the S-64F.

SIKORSKY S-65

Country of Origin: USA.
Type: Heavy assault transport helicopter.
Power Plant: Two 3,925 shp General Electric T64-GE-413 turboshafts.
Performance: Max. speed, 196 mph (315 km/h) at sea level; max. cruise, 173 mph (278 km/h); max. inclined climb, 2,180 ft/min (11,08 m/sec); hovering ceiling (in ground effect), 13,400 ft (4 080 m), (out of ground effect), 6,500 ft (1 980 m); range, 257 mls (413 km).
Weights: Empty, 23,485 lb (10 653 kg); normal take-off, 36,400 lb (16 510 kg); 42,000 lb (19 050 kg).
Dimensions: Rotor diam, 72 ft 3 in (22,02 m); fuselage length, 67 ft 2 in (20,47 m).
Notes: Using many components based on those of the S-64 (see page 247), the S-65 can accommodate 38 combat troops or 24 casualty stretchers and four medical attendants. The initial US Navy version, the CH-53A Sea Stallion, has 2,850 shp T64-GE-6 turboshafts, and the HH-53B for the USAF is similar apart from having 3,080 shp T64-GE-3s, a flight refuelling probe, jettisonable auxiliary tanks and armament, the HH-53C differing primarily in having 3,435 shp T64-GE-7s and an external cargo hook. The US Marine Corps' CH-53D (to which the specification applies) has up-rated engines and can carry up to 64 troops. The CH-53DG for Germany (illustrated) and S-65-Oe for Austria are similar.

248

SIKORSKY S-70 (YUH-60A)

Country of Origin: USA.
Type: Tactical transport helicopter.
Power Plant: Two (approx.) 1,500 shp General Electric T700-GE-700 turboshafts.
Performance: Cruising speed, 185 mph (298 km/h).
Weights: Approx. max. take-off, 15,850 lb (7 190 kg).
Dimensions: Rotor diam, 53 ft 0 in (16,15 m).
Notes: The S-70 has been selected as one of two finalists in the US Army's UTTAS (Utility Tactical Transport Aircraft System) contest as the YUH-60A, the other being the Boeing Vertol YUH-61A (see page 237), the programme calling for the manufacture of one static test specimen and three flying prototypes, the first of the latter being scheduled to commence its test programme during November 1974. The YUH-60A will accommodate four casualty stretchers plus three sitting casualties or up to 11 fully-equipped troops, and provision is made for a machine gun to be mounted in the forward cabin. The pilots will be provided with armoured seats. The YUH-60A is air-transportable—one example in a C-130 Hercules or two in a C-141A StarLifter—and features folding main and tail rotor blades, no disassembly of the airframe being required. The YUH-60A will undergo US Army trials and competitive evaluation against the YUH-61A early in 1976, and if selected will be ordered in March 1977. A company-funded example of the S-70 will fly early 1975.

WESTLAND COMMANDO MK. 2

Country of Origin: United Kingdom (US licence).
Type: Tactical transport helicopter.
Power Plant: Two 1,590 shp Rolls-Royce Gnome 1400-1 turboshafts.
Performance: Max. speed (at 19,900 lb/9 046 kg), 138 mph (222 km/h); max. cruise, 127 mph (204 km/h); max. inclined climb, 1,930 ft/min (9,8 m/sec); range (with 30 troops), 161 mls (259 km); ferry range, 1,036 mls (1 668 km).
Weights: Empty equipped, 11,487–12,122 lb (5 221–5 510 kg); max. take-off, 20,000 lb (9 072 kg).
Dimensions: Rotor diam, 62 ft 0 in (18,89 m); fuselage length, 54 ft 9 in (16,69 m).
Notes: The Commando is a Westland-developed land-based army support helicopter derivative of the licence-built Sikorsky S-61D Sea King (see page 245), search radar and other specialised items being deleted together with the sponsons which endow the Sea King with amphibious capability. The first five examples completed as Commando Mk. 1s were minimum change conversions of Sea King airframes, the first of these flying on September 12, 1973 (illustrated above), but subsequent Commandos are being built to Mk. 2 standards with the uprated Gnome turboshafts selected for the Sea King Mk. 50s ordered by Australia. The first production Commandos are being built for Egypt.

250

WESTLAND WG.13 LYNX

Country of Origin: United Kingdom.
Type: Multi-purpose and transport helicopter.
Power Plant: Two 900 shp Rolls-Royce BS.360-07-26 turboshafts.
Performance: (General purpose versions) Max. speed, 207 mph (333 km/h); max. cruise, 184 mph (296 km/h) at sea level; max. inclined climb, 2,800 ft/min (14,2 m/sec); hovering ceiling (out of ground effect), 12,000 ft (3 650 m); range (with 10 passengers), 173 mls (278 km), (with internal cargo and full tanks), 489 mls (788 km).
Weights: Operational empty, 5,532–6,125 lb (2 509–2 778 kg); max. take-off, 8,000 lb (3 620 kg); overload, 8,840 lb (4 009 kg).
Dimensions: Rotor diam, 42 ft 0 in (12,80 m); fuselage length, 38 ft 3$\frac{1}{4}$ in (11,66 m).
Notes: The Lynx, the first of 12 prototypes of which commenced its flight test programme on March 21, 1971, and the first production machine (a Lynx A.H. Mk. 1 for the British Army) was scheduled to fly at the end of 1973 with the first naval example (a Lynx HR Mk. 2 for the Royal Navy) following mid-1974. Current plans call for the delivery of some 80 examples of an ASW version to France's *Aéronavale*, the Lynx being one of three helicopter types covered by the Anglo-French agreement. A total of 277 is programmed for the British services.

ACKNOWLEDGEMENTS

The author wishes to record his thanks to the following sources of copyright photographs appearing in this volume: Miroslav Balous, 12; *Flight International*, 168, 170; K. Hinata, 190; Howard Levy, 44, 52, 114; Stephen Peltz, 20, 152, 244; H. Redemann, 56, 118, 226, 227, 236; M. West, 34. The three-view silhouettes are copyright Pilot Press Limited and must not be reproduced without prior written permission.

INDEX OF AIRCRAFT TYPES

A-4 Skyhawk, McDonnell Douglas, 144
A-6 Intruder, Grumman, 90
A-7E Corsair II, Vought, 218
A-10A, Fairchild, 78
A-37B Dragonfly, Cessna, 52
Aeritalia (Fiat) G.222, 8
-Aermacchi AM-3C, 6
Aermacchi M.B.326K, 10
Aero L 39 Albatross, 12
Aérospatiale Corvette, 14
  Rallye, 16
  SA 315B Lama, 224
  SA 316 Alouette III, 225
  SA 319 Alouette III, 225
  SA 330 Puma, 226
  SA 341 Gazelle, 227
  SA 360, 228
Aerostar, Smith, 200
Agusta A 109C Hirundo, 229
AH-1 HueyCobra, Bell, 233
Airbus A300B, 18
Airtrainer, NZAI CT-4, 160
AJ 37 Viggen, Saab, 180
Albatross, Aero L 39, 12
Alouette III, Aérospatiale, 225
Alpha Jet, Dassault-Breguet/Dornier, 68
Antonov An-24, 20
  An-26, 20
Arava, IAI-201, 114
AV-8A, Hawker Siddeley, 106
Aviocar, CASA C.212, 44

B-1A, Rockwell, 172
BAC 145 Jet Provost T. Mk. 5, 22
  167 Strikemaster, 22

One-Eleven 475, 24
-Aérospatiale Concorde, 26
Backfire (Tupolev), 204
Bandeirante, Embraer EMB-110, 76
Beechcraft B99, 28
  Super King Air 200, 30
Bell 205 Iroquois, 230
  206 JetRanger, 231
  206L Long Ranger, 232
  209 HueyCobra, 233
  212, 234
  214, 235
Blinder (Tu-22), 208
Boeing 727, 32
  737, 38
  747, 34
  E-3A, 36
  EC-137D, 36
  T-43A, 38
  Vertol 114 Chinook, 236
  Vertol YUH-61A, 237
BO 105, MBB, 241
Britten-Norman Islander, 40
  Trislander, 42
Buccaneer S. Mk. 2, Hawker Siddeley, 104
Bulldog, Scottish Aviation, 184

C-130 Hercules, Lockheed, 128
Candid (Il-76), 118
Careless (Tu-154), 214
CASA C.212 Aviocar, 44
Cayuse, Hughes OH-6A, 238
Cessna A-37B Dragonfly, 52
  Citation, 50
  Model 340, 48

T337G Pressurised Skymaster, 46
CH-3B, Sikorsky, 244
CH-3C, Sikorsky, 246
CH-47A Chinook, Boeing Vertol, 236
CH-53A Sea Stallion, Sikorsky, 248
CH-54A Tarhe, Sikorsky, 247
Cherokee Warrior, Piper, 164
Charger (Tu-144), 212
Chinook, Boeing Vertol 114, 236
Citation, Cessna, 50
Codling (Yak-40), 222
Commander 112, Rockwell, 176
Commando, Westland, 250
Concorde, BAC-Aérospatiale, 26
Corsair, Vought A-7E, 218
Corvette 100, Aérospatiale, 14
Crusty (Tu-134), 210
Curl (An-26), 20

Dassault-Breguet Falcon 10, 54
    Falcon 20, 56
    Falcon 30, 58
    Mercure, 60
    Mirage 5, 62
    Mirage F1, 64
    Super Étendard, 66
    /Dornier Alpha Jet, 68
DC-9, McDonnell Douglas, 136
DC-10, McDonnell Douglas, 138
De Havilland Canada DHC-6
    Twin Otter, 70
    DHC-7, 72
Dornier Do 28D Skyservant, 74
Dragonfly, Cessna A-37B, 52

E-2C Hawkeye, Grumman, 94
E-3A, Boeing, 36
EA-6B Prowler, Grumman, 92
Eagle, McDonnell Douglas F-15, 140
EC-137D, Boeing, 36
Embraer, EMB-110 Bandeirante, 76

F-4 Phantom, McDonnell Douglas, 142
F-5E Tiger II, Northrop, 156
F-14A Tomcat, Grumman, 96
F-15 Eagle, McDonnell Douglas, 140
F-104S Starfighter, Lockheed, 132
Fairchild A-10A, 78

Falcon 10, Dassault-Breguet, 54
    20, Dassault-Breguet, 56
    30, Dassault-Breguet, 58
Fellowship, Fokker F.28, 82
Fiat G.222, 8
Fishbed (MiG-21), 146
Flagon (Su-15), 202
Flogger (MiG-23), 148
Fokker F.27 Friendship, 80
    F.28 Fellowship, 82
Foxbat (MiG-25), 150
Friendship, Fokker F.27, 80

G.222, Aeritalia (Fiat), 8
GAF Nomad, 84
Gates Learjet 35, 86
Gazelle, Aérospatiale SA 341, 227
General Dynamics YF-16, 88
Grumman A-6 Intruder, 90
    E-2C Hawkeye, 94
    EA-6B Prowler, 92
    F-14A Tomcat, 96
Grumman American AA-5
    Traveler, 98

Hawker Siddeley 125, 100
    748, 102
    Buccaneer S. Mk. 2, 104
    Harrier, 106
    Hawk T. Mk. 1, 108
    Nimrod, 110
    Trident 2E, 112
Hawkeye, Grumman E-2C, 94
Hercules, Lockheed C-130H, 128
HH-2 Seasprite, Kaman, 239
HH-3F Pelican, Sikorsky, 246
HH-53, Sikorsky, 248
Hip (Mi-8), 242
Hirundo, Agusta A 109C, 229
Hormone (Ka-25), 240
Homer (Mi-12), 244
HueyCobra, Bell 209, 233
HueyPlus, Bell 214, 235
Hughes 500, 238

IAI-201 Arava, 114
Ilyushin Il-38 (May), 116
    Il-76 (Candid), 118
Intruder, Grumman A-6, 90
Iroquois, Bell 205A, 230
Islander, Britten-Norman, 40

JA 37 Viggen, Saab, 181
Jaguar, SEPECAT, 188

Jet Provost T. Mk. 5, BAC, 22
JetRanger, Bell 206, 231
JetStar II, Lockheed, 124
Jetstream, Scottish Aviation, 186

Kaman HH-2 Seasprite, 239
Kamov Ka-25 (Hormone), 240
Kawasaki C-1A, 120
Kiowa, Bell OH-58A, 231

Lama, Aérospatiale SA 315B, 224
Learjet 35, Gates, 86
LET L 410 Turbojet, 122
Lockheed C-130H Hercules, 128
    F-104S Starfighter, 132
    P-3C Orion, 130
    S-3A Viking, 134
    JetStar II, 124
    L-1011 TriStar, 126
Long Ranger, Bell 206L, 232
Lynx, Westland, 251

M-15, WSK-Mielec, 220
Macchi M.B.326K, 10
May (II-38), 116
MBB BO 105, 241
McDonnell Douglas A-4 Skyhawk, 144
    DC-9, 136
    DC-10, 138
    F-4 Phantom, 142
    F-15 Eagle, 140
Mercure, Dassault-Breguet, 160
MFI 15/17, Saab, 182
MiG-21MF (Fishbed), 146
MiG-23 (Flogger), 148
MiG-25 (Foxbat), 150
Mil Mi-8 (Hip), 242
    Mi-12 (Homer), 244
Mirage 5, Dassault-Breguet, 62
    F1, Dassault-Breguet, 64
Mitsubishi MU-2J, 152
    XT-2, 154
Moss (Tupolev), 206
MRCA, Panavia, 162
Mystère 10, Dassault-Breguet, 54
    20, Dassault-Breguet, 56
    30, Dassault-Breguet, 58

Nimrod, Hawker Siddeley, 110
Nomad, GAF, 84
Northrop F-5E Tiger II, 156
    YF-17, 158
NZAI CT-4 Airtrainer, 160

OH-6A Cayuse, Hughes, 238
OH-58A Kiowa, Bell, 231
One-Eleven 475, BAC, 24
Orion, Lockheed P-3C, 130

P-3C Orion, Lockheed, 130
P-530, Northrop, 158
P-600, Northrop, 158
P-630, Northrop, 158
Panavia MRCA, 162
Pelican, Sikorsky HH-3F, 246
Phantom, McDonnell Douglas F-4, 142
Piper Cherokee Warrior, 164
    Seneca, 166
Pressurised Skymaster, Cessna, 46
Prowler, Grumman EA-6B, 92

Rallye, Aérospatiale, 16
Robin HR 100-Tiara, 168
    HR 200 Acrobin, 170
    HR 200 Club, 170
Rockwell B-1A, 172
    Commander 112, 176
    Sabre 75A, 178
    XFV-12A, 174

S-3A Viking, Lockheed, 134
Saab 37 Viggen, 180
    -MFI 15/17, 182
Sabre 75A, Rockwell, 178
Scottish Aviation Bulldog, 184
    Jetstream, 186
Sea King, Sikorsky S-61D, 245
Seasprite, Kaman SH-2F, 239
Seneca, Piper PA-34, 166
SEPECAT Jaguar, 188
SH-2F Seasprite, Kaman, 239
SH-3, Sikorsky, 245
Shin Meiwa SS-2, 190
Short SD3-30, 194
    Skyvan, 192
SIAI-Marchetti SF.260W Warrior, 196
    SM.1019A, 198
Sikorsky S-61A, 244
    S-61D Sea King, 245
    S-61R, 246
    S-64 Skycrane, 247
    S-65, 248
    S-70, 249
Skycrane, Sikorsky S-64, 247
Skyhawk, McDonnell Douglas A-4, 144
Skyservant, Dornier Do 28D, 74

Skyvan, Short, 192
Smith Superstar 700, 200
Starfighter, Lockheed F-104S, 132
Strikemaster, BAC 167, 22
Sukhoi Su-15 (Flagon), 202
Super Étendard, Dassault-Breguet, 66
Super King Air 200, Beechcraft, 30
Superstar 700, Smith, 200

T-43A, Boeing, 38
Tarhe, Sikorsky CH-54A, 247
Tiger II, Northrop F-5E, 156
Tomcat, Grumman F-14A, 96
Traveler, Grumman American AA-5, 98
Trislander, Britten-Norman, 40
TriStar, Lockheed L-1011, 126
Tupolev Backfire, 204
  Moss, 206
  Tu-22 (Blinder), 208
  Tu-134 (Crusty), 210

Tu-144 (Charger), 212
Tu-154 (Careless), 214
Turbolet, LET L 410, 122
Twin Otter, de Havilland Canada, 70

VFW-Fokker VFW 614, 216
Viggen, Saab 37, 180
Viking, Lockheed S-3A, 134
Vought A-7E Corsair II, 218

Warrior, SIAI-Marchetti SF.260W, 196
Westland Commando, 250
  WG.13 Lynx, 251
WSK-Mielec M-15, 220

XFV-12A, Rockwell, 174

Yak-40 (Codling), 222
YF-16, Heneral Dynamics, 88
YF-17, Northrop, 158
YUH-60A, Sikorsky, 249
YUH-61A, Boeing Vertol, 237

Printed for the Publishers by
Butler & Tanner Ltd, Frome and London

1366.1073